Crossroads Café

PHOTO STORIES B

The publication of *Crossroads Café* was directed by the members of the Heinle & Heinle Secondary and Adult ESL Publishing Team.

Editorial Director:	Roseanne Mendoza
Senior Production Services Coordinator:	Lisa McLaughlin
Market Development Director:	Andy Martin

Also participating in the publication of the program were:

Vice President and Publisher, ESL:	Stanley Galek
Developmental Editor:	Sally Conover
Production Editor:	Maryellen Killeen
Manufacturing Coordinator:	Mary Beth Hennebury
Director of Global ELT Training and Development:	Evelyn Nelson
Full Service Design and Production:	PC&F, Inc.

Manufactured in the United States of America.

ISBN: 0-8384-66079

Heinle & Heinle is a division of International Thomson Publishing, Inc.

Photo Credits
Episodes 1, 2, 3, 4, 5, 6, 9, 10, 13, 14, 16, 17, 18: Stanley Newton
Episodes 7, 8, 11, 12, 15, 19, 20, 21, 22, 23, 24, 25, 26: Jane O'Neal
Episode 15, pages 33 and 34: K. Lynn Savage

Crossroads Café

PHOTO STORIES B

K. Lynn Savage • Patricia Mooney Gonzalez
with Edwina Hoffman

HEINLE & HEINLE PUBLISHERS
I T P *An International Thomson Publishing Company*
Boston, Massachusetts 02116 U.S.A.

New York • London • Bonn • Boston • Detroit • Madrid • Melbourne • Mexico City • Paris •
Singapore • Tokyo • Toronto • Washington • Albany, NY • Belmont, CA • Cincinnati, OH

Acknowledgments

Rigorous review by members of the National Academic Council contributed to the initial design as well as the philosophical underpinnings of the products: Fiona Armstrong, Office of Adult and Continuing Education, New York City Board of Education; Janet Buongiorno, Adult Literacy Enhancement Center, Edison, New Jersey; Yvonne Cadiz, Adult and Community Education Program, Hillsborough County Public Schools, Florida; the late Jim Dodd, Bureau of Adult and Community Education, Department of Education, Florida; Chela Gonzalez, Metropolitan Adult Education Program, San Jose, California; Chip Harman, United States Information Agency, Washington, D.C.; Edwina Hoffman, Dade County Public Schools, Florida; Maggie Steinz, Illinois State Board of Education; Dennis Terdy, Adult Learning Resource Center, Des Plaines, Illinois; Inaam Mansour, Arlington Education and Employment Program, Arlington, Virginia; Fortune Valenty, Perth Amboy Public Schools, New Jersey; Kathleen Santopietro Weddel, Colorado Department of Education.

Collaboration among the Institute for Social Research at the University of Michigan, Interwest Applied Research in Portland, Oregon, and the National Center for Adult Literacy provided evaluation data that guided modification of student materials and development of teacher/tutor materials. Guiding and directing the evaluations were Jere Johnston, Dan Wagner, Regie Stites, and Evelyn Brzezinski. Participating pilot sites included the following: Alhambra School District, California; The Brooklyn Adult Learning Center, New York City Board of Education; Dade County Public Schools, Florida; Mt. Hood Community College, Portland, Oregon; Jewish Family Services, San Diego, California; Polish Welfare Association, Chicago, Illinois; One-Stop Immigration Center, Los Angeles, California; Even Start Program, Northside Independent School District, San Antonio, Texas; Margarita R. Huantes, Learning and Leadership Development Center, San Antonio, Texas; San Diego Community College District.

The collaboration with INTELECOM resulted in provocative stories, which provided meaningful contexts for the *Worktext's* activities. Thank you to Sarah for graciously providing whatever was needed and holding everything together during the most frenetic stages of the project; Peter and Glenn for providing entertaining and relevant story lines; Bob for keeping everyone properly focused; and Sally, for her leadership as well as her commitment and involvement in all aspects of the project.

Extensive experience of Heinle & Heinle and its staff in publishing language-learning materials ensured quality print materials. The authors wish to thank Nancy Mann, *Worktexts* editor, for her professionalism and expertise; Sally Conover, *Photo Stories* editor, for the dedication, patience, and attention to detail that the Photo Stories required; Lisa McLaughlin, production coordinator, for ensuring that the extremely tight production schedule was met without sacrificing quality; Maryellen Killeen, production editor, for her infinite patience and good humor in sorting through the hundreds of photos for the Photo Stories; Roseanne Mendoza, acquisitions editor, for her willingness to take the risks that the development of cutting edge products requires and for her commitment to fighting for the things she believes in.

Table of Contents

Photo Story B

SCANS* AT-A-GLAN

Video Time (min: sec) Worktext	Crossroads Café Lesson Plans	SCANS Discussion Focus
14 Life Goes On		
• 1:22–2:49 • 5:30–7:56 Text p. 13 • Text p. 12	• Managing the café during Mr. Brashov's hospitalization • Culture Clip: Hospitals • What Do You Think?	• Interpersonal: *teamwork* • Systems: *understand organizational systems* • Information: *interpret*
15 Breaking Away		
• 3:55–6:28 21:23–24:14 • 8:17–12:13 Text p. 27 • Text p. 26	• Preparing for rejection Henry's parents and his girl friend's parents meet. • Culture Clip: Intercultural Relationships • What Do You Think?	• Personal: *self esteem* • Thinking: *solve problems* • Sociability: *understanding adaptability* • Interpersonal: *persuade*
16 The Bottom Line		
• 4:22–5:21 • 12:55–14:17 • 15:29–17:12 • Text p. 40	• Mr. Brashov tries to apply for a loan • The banker visits the restaurant. • Word Play: Reporting Information • What Do You Think?	• Systems: *monitor and correct performance* • Thinking: *recognize problem, create a plan of action* • Basic Skills: *organize and communicate ideas* • Thinking: *solve problems*
17 United We Stand		
• 15:22–15:59 • 6:16–8:40 Text p. 55 • Text p. 54	• Rosa organizes a tenants' meeting. • Culture Clip: Tenant and Landlord Responsibilities • What Do You Think?	• Thinking: *recognize problems, devise action plan* • Systems: *work within the system* • Systems: *organizational systems*
18 Opportunity Knocks		
• 4:57–7:54 • 17:51–20:21 Text p. 69 • Text p. 68	• Jamal is offered a job. • Culture Clip: Worker Safety • What Do You Think?	• Personal: *choose ethical courses of action* • Systems: *understand and operate effectively* • Personal: *integrity*
19 The People's Choice		
• 3:15–5:54 • 9:44–12:10 Text p. 83 • Text p. 82	• Jess runs for City Council. • Culture Clip: Local Government • What Do You Think?	• Personal: *self-worth* • Systems: *understand organizational systems* • Information: *evaluate*

*****SCANS** is an acronym for the Secretary's Commission on Achieving Necessary Skills (U.S. Department of Labor, 1991)

Video Time (min: sec) Worktext	Crossroads Café Lesson Plans	SCANS Discussion Focus
20 Outside Looking In		
• 24:38–25:39 • 16:28–19:30 Text p. 97 • Text p. 96	• Rosa translates at a business party • Culture Clip: Raising Children • What Do You Think?	• Basic Skills: *speaking—communicates orally* • Interpersonal: *cultural diversity* • Personal: *self worth*
21 Walls and Bridges		
• 12:19–14:22 • 22:48–25:31 • 18:55–22:16 Text p. 111 • Text p. 110	• Rosa and Chris go to Mr. Hernandez's tailor shop. • Talking about daughters. • Culture Clip: Becoming a Citizen • What Do You Think?	• Interpersonal: *negotiate* • Interpersonal Skills: *teach others new skills* • Systems: *understand organizational system* • Thinking: *solve problems*
22 Helping Hands		
• 21:21–24:11 • 7:10–9:57 Text p. 125 • Text p. 124	• Helping Frank get a job • Culture Clip: Financial Difficulties • What Do You Think?	• Thinking: *think creatively* • Resources: *allocate money to meet objectives* • Information: *interpret and communicate*
23 The Gift		
• 22:58–25:06 • 10:48–12:47 Text p. 139 • Text p. 138	• Planning Mr. Brashov's surprise birthday party • Culture Clip: Taxes • What Do You Think?	• Thinking: *think creatively* and *make decisions* • Systems: *understand social systems* • Information: *analyze and communicate*
24 All's Well That Ends Well		
• 8:01–10:20 Text p. 153 • Text p. 152	• Culture Clip: Wedding Customs • What Do You Think?	• Interpersonal: *cultural diversity* • Interpersonal: *communicate ideas to justify position*
25 Comings and Goings		
• 8:26–9:57 • 9:59–11:48 Text p. 167 • Text p. 166	• Jamal receives job offer • Culture Clip: Returning to Your Home Culture • What Do You Think?	• Personal: *assess self, set goals* • Thinking: *solve problems* • Interpersonal: *persuade*
26 Winds of Change		
• 11:43–15:18 Text p. 181	• Culture Clip: Achieving Goals	• Personal: *set personal goals*
• Text p. 180	• What Do You Think?	• Personal: *set personal goals*

To the Learner: About *Crossroads Café*

These pages explain what the *Crossroads Café* program is and how to use it. If you have problems understanding these explanations, ask someone to read and discuss them with you. If you start with a clear idea of how to use *Crossroads Café* correctly, your chances for success will be great.

Crossroads Café provides a unique method to learn English. The use of a television series and videos will help you improve your English. The *Crossroads Café* books are excellent tools for helping you use the television series or the videos to improve your listening, speaking, reading, and writing in English. The next section explains how each piece of the program can help you. It also answers some important questions about the series and how it should be used.

What Is *Crossroads Café?*

Crossroads Café is a course for studying English. The course teaches English as it entertains. It also helps you understand North American culture and use that understanding to live and work in the culture more successfully.

What Are the Parts of the Program?

There are three parts of the program for learners.
- The 26 television programs or the videos
- The two *Photo Stories* books
- The two *Worktexts*

You will use television programs or videos with the *Photo Stories,* the *Worktexts,* or both to learn English.

What Are the Television Programs?

The television programs are the most important part of the *Crossroads Café* program. There are 26 thirty-minute episodes that tell the story of a group of hard-working, determined people whose lives come together at a small neighborhood restaurant called Crossroads Café. Some of them are newcomers to the United States. Others have families that have been here for one or many generations. These people slowly create a successful neighborhood restaurant. During the 26 episodes, *Crossroads Café* tells of the successes and the failures, the joys and the sadness, and especially the learning experiences of the owner of the café, the people who work in it, their families, friends, acquaintances, neighbors, and the people they must cooperate with to be successful in their work and in their lives. The story is sometimes funny, sometimes sad, but always entertaining. The large picture above shows the six main characters in *Crossroads Café*. The smaller pictures around it show the characters in their lives outside the café.

These are the people you will learn about in *Crossroads Café*. You will be able to understand many of the problems they face and share many of their feelings. You will learn from their experiences—learn English and learn something about North American culture. You will also discover new ways to learn—which can be new paths to success for you in an English-speaking culture.

Most of each thirty-minute program deals with the story of the café and its six characters. But there are two other pieces in each episode that are especially good for people who want to learn English and understand North American culture. In every episode, there is a short section called "Word Play." "Word Play" always shows and explains some special way English is used in that episode. It combines cartoons, illustrations, and scenes from the episode to teach how to use English for a special purpose. For example, "Word Play" presents ways to ask for help, make suggestions, or, as this picture shows, make complaints.

The second special section that is part of every episode is the "Culture Clip." It helps you understand North American culture. You can agree or disagree with the behavior the "Culture Clip" shows, but this section will always help you think about your ideas on culture, in your own country and in your life today. This can help you understand and deal with cultural differences.

How Do I Use the Television Programs or Videos?

You can use the program if you are any of these types of learner. Here's how each type can best use the television programs or the videos.

1. **The Independent Learner.** You want to study the language on your own—possibly with the help of a tutor, a friend, a neighbor, or a family member. You may have seen an episode of *Crossroads Café* on television, or you may have heard about it from someone else—a friend or a family member. You may have seen ads for the program in a store or a library. You ordered the *Crossroads Café* program on your own because you wanted to learn English at home, by yourself or with someone else.

2. **The Distant Learner.** You study in a distance-learning program in a school. You may talk to or see your teacher once a week, once every two weeks, or once a month. But most of your study will be done alone, using the *Crossroads Café* materials. Your teacher may tell you to watch *Crossroads Café* one or more times each week and do the activities in the *Worktexts*, the *Photo Stories*, or both. When you meet with your teacher—and perhaps with other students too—you will talk about what you saw and learned. You may also do some activities from the *Teacher's Resource Book* with the other students and your teacher.

3. The Classroom Learner. You study in a regular class with a teacher in a school. You will use the *Crossroads Café* books—*Worktexts, Photo Stories,* or both—in your class. Your teacher will ask you to watch *Crossroads Café* programs and do some of the activities in your book at home. In class, you will work with other students to do more activities in the *Worktext* or the *Photo Stories* and other activities from the *Teacher's Resource Book.* Your teacher may also show important pieces of the episodes again in class and discuss them with the students.

How Do I Use the *Worktexts?*

Each of the two *Crossroads Café Worktexts* contains thirteen episodes—half the episodes in the complete series. Every *Worktext* lesson has the same parts, which you will use to practice and improve your English before and after you watch the television or video.

The *Worktexts* are carefully written to help learners at three different levels of English study—high beginning, low intermediate, and high intermediate. You can "grow" with the program by using the same *Worktexts* and videos over and over as you acquire more English. Here's how these multi-level *Worktexts* can work for you.

The different activities in each section of the books are marked with colored stars—one, two, or three stars for the three different levels of learners. Here are two possible ways to use the *Worktexts.*

1. If you are working alone, without a teacher, try to work through all three levels in the first unit to see which level suits you best. Be honest with yourself. If you check your answers and see that you've made mistakes at a certain level, it's best to choose the level below that one. If you have a teacher or a tutor, he or she will probably choose a level for you. After you know your level, always do the activities for that level, as well as the activities for the levels before it. For example, let's say you decide you are a two-star learner. In every section, you will do the one-star activity first and then the two-star activity. If you are a three-star learner, you will do the one-star and the two-star activities before you do the three-star activity. Don't skip the lower-level activities. They are the warm-up practice that can help you succeed when you reach your own level.

2. In each section, go as far as you can in the star system. For example, in the first activity in an episode, you may be able to do both the one-star and the two-star activities easily. However, you may not be able to complete the three-star activity. So, stop after the two-star activity and move on to the next section. In the second section, you may be able to all three levels of stars easily, or you may only be able to do the one-star activity. Always begin with the one-star activity and, if you succeed, then move on to the more advanced activities. If you have problems with an activity, get help right away from your teacher or tutor, or from someone whose English is better than yours.

Remember, if you are studying alone you can choose one of those two ways of working. If you have a teacher or a tutor, that person can help you decide how to work. But if you have problems with any activity, always try to get help immediately from your teacher, your tutor, or someone else who knows more English than you. That way, you can understand what to do and how to correct yourself.

How Can the *Worktext* Activities Help Me Learn?

The *Worktext* activities do three things:

1. They help you understand the story on the video.
2. They provide language practice.
3. They ask you to think about, talk about, and write about your ideas.

Understanding the Story: To help you understand the story, the *Worktext* has activities for you to do before and after you watch the episode.

Before you watch, you can do three things:

- Look at the big picture on the first page for the episode. Look at the title. Then try to guess what the story is about. Talk about your ideas with someone.
- Then look at the six pictures in the "Before You Watch" section. Talk about the pictures with someone. Do the exercises that go with the pictures. Check your answers by looking at the answer key in the back of the book.
- Finally, read the questions in the "Focus for Watching" section. If you do not understand some words, use your dictionary, or ask someone what the words mean.

After you watch the episode, turn to the "After You Watch" activities in your *Worktext*. In these activities, you will do two things:

- You will match key people from the story with the focus questions.
- You will answer questions about important parts of the story and then you will put those parts in order.

Practicing the Language helps you develop your English language skills. This section of the *Worktext* gives you special activities to do after you watch the television or video. These next three sections will help you improve your grammar, your reading, and your writing.

Your New Language presents grammar for a special purpose. For example, you will learn to use commands to tell someone to do something. Or you will learn to use *can* and *know how to* to talk about what you are able to do. Here is a good way to do these activities:

- Watch "Word Play" on the video again, if possible.
- Complete the "Your New Language" section of your *Worktext*.
- Check your answers. Use the "Answer Key" in the back of the *Worktexts*.
- Practice the conversations in "Your New Language" with someone.

In Your Community presents the kind of reading you find in your everyday life. Here is a good way to do these activities:

- Answer the questions about the reading.
- Check your answers. Use the "Answer Key" in the back of your *Worktext*.
- Look for the same kind of reading in the town or city where you live.
- Compare the reading you find with the one in the *Worktext*.

Read and Write presents something that a person in *Crossroads Café* wrote. It may be a letter, a note, a diary page, or a newspaper article. Here is a good way to do these activities:

- Answer the questions about the main ideas of the writing.
- Guess the meaning of the words in the vocabulary exercises.
- Use your experiences to write about something similar.
- Share your writing with someone.

Two sections of each *Worktext* unit have exercises that ask you to give your opinions about something that happened in the story. These sections are called "What Do You Think?" and "Culture Clip."

Here is a good way to work through the **What Do You Think?** activities:

- Think about things people in the story have done or opinions they have expressed.
- Share your ideas with someone.

Here is a good way to work through the **Culture Clip** activities:

- Watch the "Culture Clip" on the video again, if possible.
- Identify the main ideas from the "Culture Clip."
- Give your own opinion about a situation related to the "Culture Clip."

Check Your English is the last activity in each unit. It is a review of vocabulary, grammar, and reading. You can check your answers with the "Answer Key" in the back of your *Worktext*.

What Are the *Photo Stories?*

The *Crossroads Café Photo Stories* do these things:

- They help you understand the story before you watch the video.
- They ask you questions to help you understand parts of the story.
- They help you improve your vocabulary.
- They help you review after you watch.

The *Photo Stories* can help you if you know a little English or a lot of English:

- They can be special books for beginning learners of English. Learners study the pictures from the video. These pictures have the words from the story in them. This combination of words and photos makes learning English easy. If you speak Spanish, you may have read *fotonovelas,* or *telefotonovelas.* The *Photo Stories* look very much like those books, and they tell interesting stories, too.

- They are also for more advanced students of English. They can be an extra help for you if you are using the *Worktexts.* You can use the *Photo Story* to preview each television or video episode. First read the *Photo Story* and then do the exercises. Then, when you watch the episode, you will be prepared to understand what is happening and know what the characters will say.

This sample page shows how the *Photo Stories* tell the story of the video and help you read to find the meaning.

This sample page shows one type of activity you will do after you read the story.

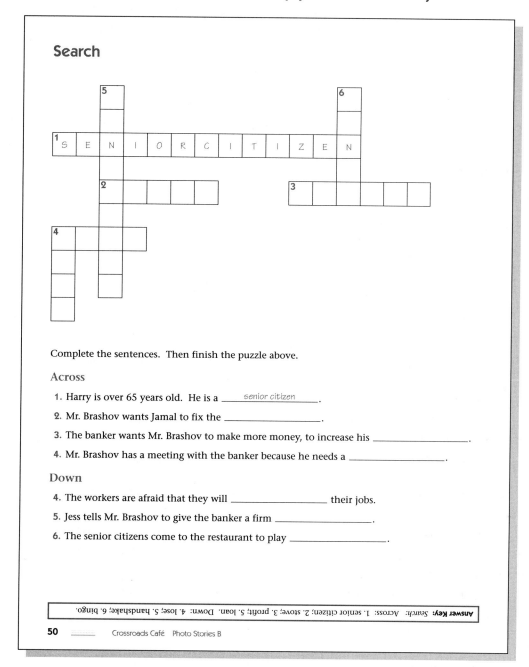

Search

Complete the sentences. Then finish the puzzle above.

Across

1. Harry is over 65 years old. He is a _____ senior citizen _____.
2. Mr. Brashov wants Jamal to fix the _____.
3. The banker wants Mr. Brashov to make more money, to increase his _____.
4. Mr. Brashov has a meeting with the banker because he needs a _____.

Down

4. The workers are afraid that they will _____ their jobs.
5. Jess tells Mr. Brashov to give the banker a firm _____.
6. The senior citizens come to the restaurant to play _____.

Special Questions about *Crossroads Café*

Learners of English and their teachers and tutors sometimes ask these questions about *Crossroads Café*.

What if I can't understand everything in the television or video episodes? Don't worry if you can't understand some language in the episodes. Even if you don't understand a lot of language, you can still learn from watching. You will often be able to guess what is happening in the story. This is because sometimes the people use actions that help you understand the meaning of their words. Also, sometimes they will look happy, surprised, or even angry when they speak. These facial expressions help you guess what they are saying. Learn to watch for these clues. They can help you understand the story. Good language learners know how to use these clues to help themselves. With *Crossroads Café*, you will learn to develop successful language-learning habits.

What if I can't understand the way some of the characters speak? In *Crossroads Café*, several important characters were either born in the U.S. or arrived when they were very young. They speak English without accents:

- Katherine is from the Midwest.
- Jess is from the South.
- Henry was born in China, but immigrated to the U.S. before he started school.

But some characters are from other parts of the world:

- Mr. Brashov is from Eastern Europe.
- Rosa was born in the U.S., but she grew up in Latin America.
- Jamal is from the Middle East.

These characters, like you, are still improving their English pronunciation, although they always use correct grammar. It will help you to hear many different pronunciations of English. In North America, and in the world in general, people speak English in many different ways. In schools, at work, and in the streets, other people need to understand them to communicate successfully with them. Becoming accustomed to hearing speakers from different cultures and different ethnic groups is a skill successful English speakers need to develop in our modern world.

What if the English is too fast for me? In *Crossroads Café*, the characters speak at a natural speed. Their speech is not artificially slow. In the real world, very few people talk slowly to help learners of English, so in *Crossroads Café* you will hear English spoken naturally. This will be helpful to you in the long run. But the *Crossroads Café* course can give you extra help as you become accustomed to hearing English at a normal pace. Here are four ways you can use the program to get this help:

- You can preview and review the story by using the *Photo Stories*, the *Worktext*, or both.
- If you meet with your teacher and your class, your teacher may use the video version to show again some important pieces of the episode you already watched.
- Your teacher may also show some pieces of a video episode *before* you see the complete episode at home on television.
- You can record complete episodes of *Crossroads Café* with a VCR and then play them back for yourself again and again. Or you may want to buy some or all of the video episodes by calling 1-800-ESL-BY-TV (1-800-375-2988) or 1-800-354-9706.

Why should I have a study partner? Learning a language means learning to communicate with others. Using videos and television programs to learn a language has many advantages, but seeing the programs and doing the reading, writing, and thinking activities in the *Worktext* is not enough. Having a study partner gives you the opportunity to practice your new language skills. That person can be another *Crossroads Café* English learner. It can be a wonderful shared experience to do the lessons and watch the videos with a partner who is also learning English. But your partner could also be someone who knows more English than you do. It can be someone who is not studying with the *Crossroads Café* materials—someone like a relative who knows English and can help you—perhaps a son or a daughter, a husband or a wife, or any other family member. Or the partner can be a neighbor, a person who works with you, a friend, or any person who knows more English than you do. And, finally, the partner can be a formal or informal tutor—a librarian, a high-school student, or someone who used to be a teacher. Any of these people can help make the time you spend learning English more productive. If your partner knows more English than you do, he or she can use the *Crossroads Café Partner Guide*. The *Partner Guide* is small and easy to use, but it has excellent ideas for helping learners of English.

Crossroads Café—Summaries of Units 1 to 13

1 Opening Day — Victor Brashov is ready to open a new restaurant, but the restaurant doesn't have a name or workers.

2 Growing Pains — Henry has problems with working at the café. A health and safety inspector visits the café.

3 Worlds Apart — Rosa's boyfriend arrives from Mexico, and she must make a difficult decision. Mr. Brashov has trouble sleeping.

4 Who's the Boss? — Jamal sees two old friends. They think he's the owner of the café.

5 Lost and Found — Katherine's son has behavior problems in school. He gets help from someone. Jess and Carol's house is robbed.

6 Time is Money — An efficiency expert comes to look at the café. Rosa has problems with her night school class.

7 Fish Out of Water — Mr. Brashov's brother arrives from Romania. He finds that life in the United States is different from life in his country.

8 Family Matters — Katherine takes a second job to make more money. Rosa teaches Henry to dance.

9 Rush to Judgment — Jamal is a suspect in a robbery. Henry's grandparents get lost in the city.

10 Let the Buyer Beware — Mr. Brashov meets a woman who promises to improve the café's business. He goes out on several dates with her. Katherine also goes out on a date.

11 No Vacancy — Rosa wants to move into a new apartment, but she has problems. Henry works on a journalism project.

12 Turning Points — Someone breaks into the café. Rosa learns to drive.

13 Trading Places — The café employees change jobs for a day. Jess and Carol have problems at home.

14 Life Goes On

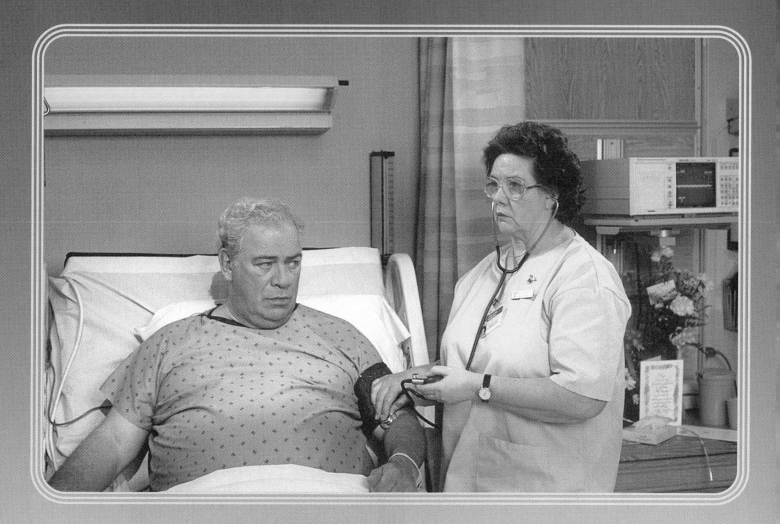

Mr. Brashov is in the hospital. While he is sick, there are changes at the café. There are changes with his family, too.

What are the changes?

Who's in This Story?

Victor Brashov
the café owner

Brenda
a nurse

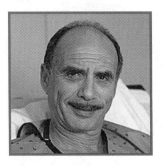

Joe Jenkins
a patient

Anna Brashov
Mr. Brashov's daughter

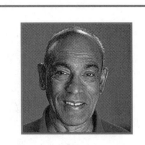

Jess
a regular customer

Jamal
the handyman

Rosa
the cook

Henry
the busboy and
delivery person

Katherine
the waitress

1

2

3

4

5

6

7

8

9

10

11

12

13

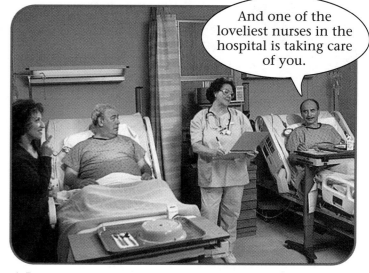

14

15

16

17

18

19 We will take care of everything.

Who will phone in the orders? Who will check the deliveries?

20 Can you get my insurance policy? Here's the combination to the safe.

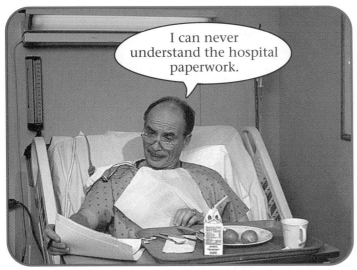

21 I can never understand the hospital paperwork.

22 I have to go.

Thanks for everything.

23 Don't worry about the café, Mr. Brashov.

24 Good-bye, Mr. Jenkins.

See you again.

3. Who comes to visit Mr. Brashov?

  a. Jess

  b. Rosa

4. What does Mr. Brashov want Rosa
to do?

  a. look for his health insurance policy

  b. be the boss at the café

25

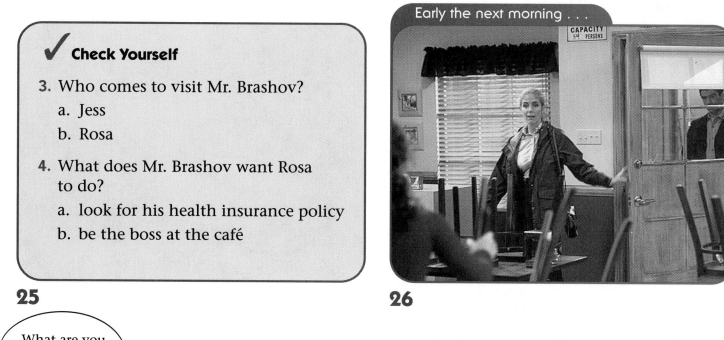

Early the next morning . . .

26

What are you
all doing here?
You're early.

We're here to
make sure that the café
opens as usual.

27

You
know what
Mr. Brashov
would say?

Yes, I'm not
paying you overtime
for this.

28

How is
Mr. Brashov
doing?

The nurse says
he's doing fine.

29

I'm going to
look for something for
Mr. Brashov.

30

Rosa begins to give orders.

31 Let's all get to work. Henry, take the chairs down. Jamal, fill the salt and pepper shakers. Katherine, set the tables.

32 Time out! Who made you the boss?

I'm sure that's what Mr. Brashov would want.

33 I can't work here if you are the boss.

And I can't work here if you are the boss.

34 What about Jamal?

My wife is out of town. I have to take care of the baby.

35 Henry is too young to be the boss.

Maybe Jess could manage the café.

36 How long will Victor be away?

A couple of weeks.

37

38

39

40

41

42

43

44

45

46

47

48

49

50

51

52

53

54

55

56

57

✓ **Check Yourself**

7. Who leaves something at the café for Mr. Brashov?
   a. his brother
   b. his daughter

8. Why doesn't Anna go to see Mr. Brashov?
   a. She and her father do not talk.
   b. She doesn't have time.

58

59

60

61

62

63

64

65

66

A few days later . . .

I have something for you.

A bill that we didn't pay?

No, it's not a bill.

67

What's this? A welcome-home present from you?

No, this is from someone else.

68

Mr. Brashov looks at a picture.

I don't understand.

There's a card with it.

69

Mr. Brashov reads the card.

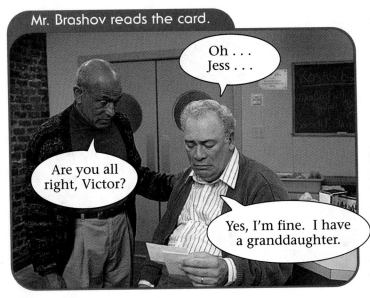

Oh . . . Jess . . .

Are you all right, Victor?

Yes, I'm fine. I have a granddaughter.

70

She has my eyes, my nose. I just hope she doesn't have my appetite.

She's a very pretty little girl, Victor.

71

✓ **Check Yourself**

9. What is in the package for Mr. Brashov?
   a. a picture
   b. a book

10. What does the card tell Mr. Brashov?
    a. that he has a son
    b. that he has a granddaughter

72

Tell the Story

Put the pictures and sentences in order. Number 1 to 5. Then tell the story to someone.

___ a.

Anna leaves a package at the café.

_1_ b.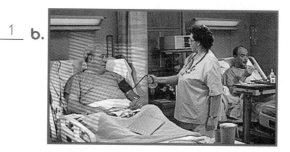

Mr. Brashov is a patient in the hospital.

___ c.

Mr. Brashov shows Jess a picture
of his granddaughter.

___ d.

Jess does Mr. Brashov's job at the café.

___ e.

Mr. Brashov comes back to the café.

Search

Complete the sentences. Then finish the puzzle above.

Across

1. There are many _____patients_____ in the hospital.

3. Mr. Brashov has to go to the _____.

6. Joe Jenkins _____ in the operating room.

Down

2. The _____ takes care of Mr. Brashov.

4. Anna leaves a _____ at the café.

5. Mr. Brashov does not like the hospital _____.

Build Your Vocabulary

A Hospital Room

Read the words in the list. Find the numbers in the picture.

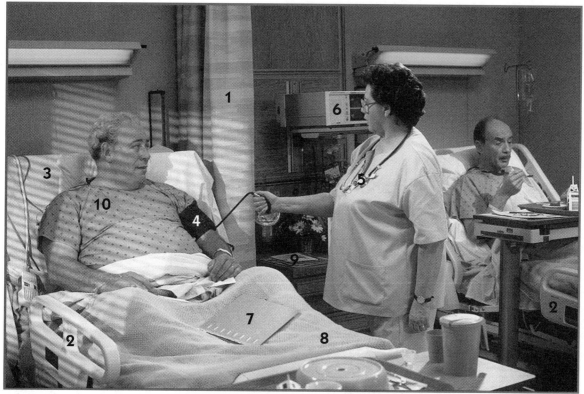

1. curtain
2. bedrails
3. hospital bed
4. blood pressure cuff
5. stethoscope
6. heart monitor
7. chart
8. blanket
9. get well card
10. hospital gown

Complete the sentences. Use the words from the picture.

1. Mr. Brashov is wearing a ___hospital gown (10)___ .

2. Brenda writes information on the patient's _____.

3. The nurse puts a _____ around the patient's arm.

4. The nurse uses a _____ to listen to a patient's heart.

5. _____ keep the patient from falling out of bed.

6. It was cold last night, so Mr. Brashov asked for another _____.

7. A _____ is a machine that gives information about a patient's heart.

8. Mr. Brashov doesn't like to sleep in a _____.

9. Everyone at the café signs a _____ for Mr. Brashov.

10. When a patient wants to be alone, the nurse pulls the _____ around the bed.

Picture Dictionary

Study the picture and the English word. Copy the word. Then you may write the word in your language.

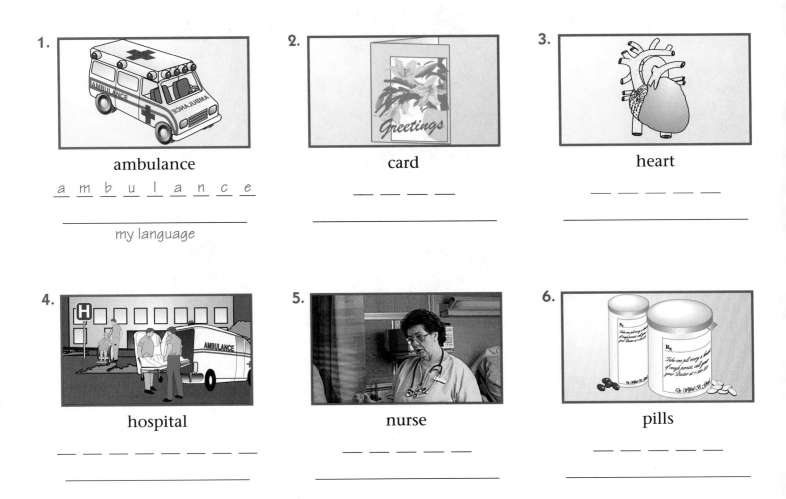

1. ambulance

a m b u l a n c e

my language

2. card

_ _ _ _

3. heart

_ _ _ _ _

4. hospital

_ _ _ _ _ _ _ _

5. nurse

_ _ _ _ _

6. pills

_ _ _ _ _

Glossary

heart attack: a sudden failure of the heart sometimes with chest pain and breathing trouble. _Every year many people in the United States die from heart attacks._

manage: to take care of something. _The record store owner wants someone to manage the business when he goes on vacation._

organized: well planned or arranged. _The student has to be organized or he won't do well in school._

overtime: time that employees work more than their regular hours. _Most people get paid more money each hour for working overtime._

strict: expecting rules to be followed. _The music teacher is very strict about how long his students must practice._

15 Breaking Away

Henry and Sara are going out with each other. Sara wants to tell her parents. Henry doesn't want to tell his parents.

What happens when the parents find out?

Who's in This Story?

Henry Chang
the café delivery person
a high school student

Sara Grayson
Henry's classmate
and friend

Mrs. Chang
Henry's mother

Mr. Chang
Henry's father

Edward Chang
Henry's brother

Gail Grayson
Sara's mother

Dick Grayson
Sara's father

Linda Blasco
owner of laundromat
next to the café

Jess
a regular customer

Victor Brashov
the café owner

Jamal
the handyman

Rosa
the cook

Katherine
the waitress

19 You don't have to go. Just tell them this is important.

My dinner with Sara is important. We're going to tell her parents that we are going together.

20 Be prepared for disappointment.

I don't understand.

21 They will be very nice. They will ask you about Chinese food. They will ask you about China. Then they will ask you not to go with their daughter.

22 They won't want Sara to date you because you are Chinese.

I think you are wrong.

✔ **Check Yourself**

3. Mrs. Chang wants Henry to have dinner with
   a. the Graysons and their daughter Sara
   b. the Fongs and their daughter Karen

4. Mrs. Chang thinks the Graysons will be
   a. happy about Henry's news
   b. unhappy about Henry's news

23

24 Several days later at the café . . .

Mr. Brashov, the building next door is going to be a laundromat.

I don't like that. The customers will come here for change. But they won't buy anything.

25 A few minutes later . . .

Jamal, there is no water. See what is wrong.

26 A woman enters the café.

Can I have change for a dollar?

Certainly.

27 I need to call the Department of Water and Power. We turned off the water, but it is still coming out.

You shut off **my** water.

28 You mean we turned off the wrong valve? Sorry . . . Let me introduce myself. I'm Linda Blasco.

29 Now I don't need to make that phone call.

30 What did I tell you? People from the laundromat are already asking for change.

Don't judge her so quickly. She seems nice.

37

Shouldn't you wait? We have many plans for our daughter. I'm sure your parents have plans for you.

38

You don't want us to be together.

We are asking you to wait for a while.

39

You don't approve of me. Excuse me. I think I'd better leave.

40

41

Several days later at Crossroads Café . . .

What am I going to do, Jamal? Every time I call Sara, she hangs up.

You have a problem.

42

You are asking Sara to choose between her family and you.

I am asking her to understand my side. She saw how her mother and father treated me.

43

You think they don't approve of you because you are Chinese. But maybe they think your hair is too long. Maybe they think you have bad manners.

44

How do your parents feel about this?

They would be happier if Sara were Chinese.

45

I have an idea. You can get your parents together with Sara's parents. All of you can talk about your problem.

46

Linda enters the café . . .

Did you just lose power?

Look around.

Right. The lights are out. Sorry about that.

47

✓ **Check Yourself**

7. Henry has a problem because
   a. Sara won't talk to him
   b. He doesn't like Linda

8. Henry thinks his parents are
   a. happy about Sara
   b. unhappy about Sara

48

Several days later at Crossroads Café . . .

Henry, why are we here?

49

50

51

52

53

54

55
56

57
58

59

Check Yourself

9. Henry apologizes to the Graysons
   a. because he was rude
   b. because he is Chinese

10. Mr. Chang and Mr. Grayson agree
    a. that Sara and Henry can marry
    b. that they can trust Sara and Henry

Tell the Story

Match the picture with the sentence. Then tell the story to someone.

1.

2.

3.

4.

5.

6.

a. Mrs. Chang tells Henry that the Graysons won't want Sara to go out with a Chinese boy.

b. Henry tells the workers at Crossroads Café that he and Sara are going together.

c. Henry has dinner at the Graysons.

d. Henry brings his parents and the Graysons together to talk.

e. Henry becomes angry and leaves the dinner.

f. Jamal gives Henry advice.

Search

For each sentence in the box, write the number in a circle.

> 1. Sara and Henry are going together.
>
> 2. The Changs would like Henry to have a Chinese girlfriend.
>
> 3. The Graysons don't approve of Henry.
>
> 4. Mr. and Mrs. Grayson have many plans for Sara.
>
> 5. Sara wants to tell her parents that she and Henry are going together.
>
> 6. The Graysons are prejudiced.

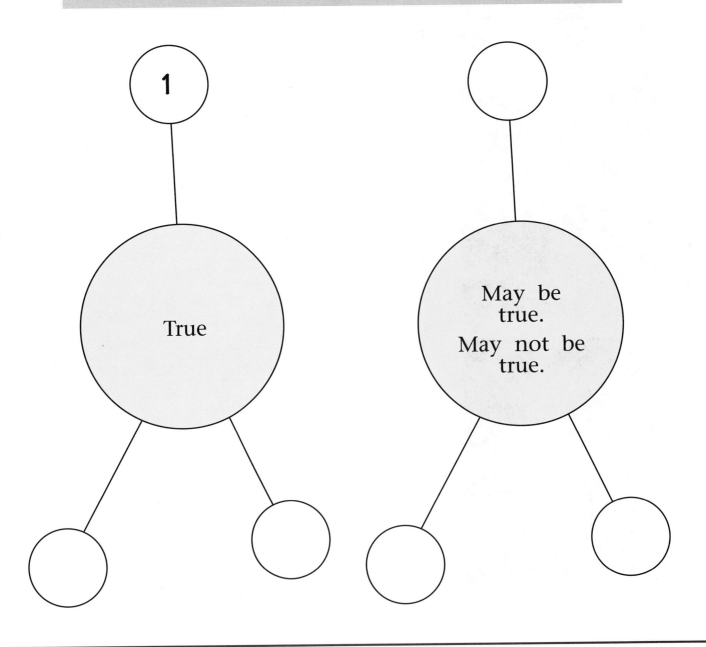

Build Your Vocabulary

The Laundromat

Read the words in the list. Find the numbers in the picture.

1. laundry basket
2. dirty clothes
3. change machine
4. washers
5. coin slot
6. dryers
7. bleach
8. laundry soap

Complete the sentences. Use the words from the picture.

1. Customers can get change for a dollar from the ___change machine (3)___.

2. The _____ for washing clothes are in the middle of the room.

3. The 4 _____, machines for drying clothes, are on the wall.

4. To run the machines, put quarters in the _____.

5. The _____ in the box will get your clothes clean.

6. The _____ in the bottle next to the box will make your clothes white.

7. There are _____ on the washing machine.

8. There is a _____ for moving wet clothes from the washer to the dryer.

Picture Dictionary

Study the picture and the English word. Copy the word. Then you may write the word in your language.

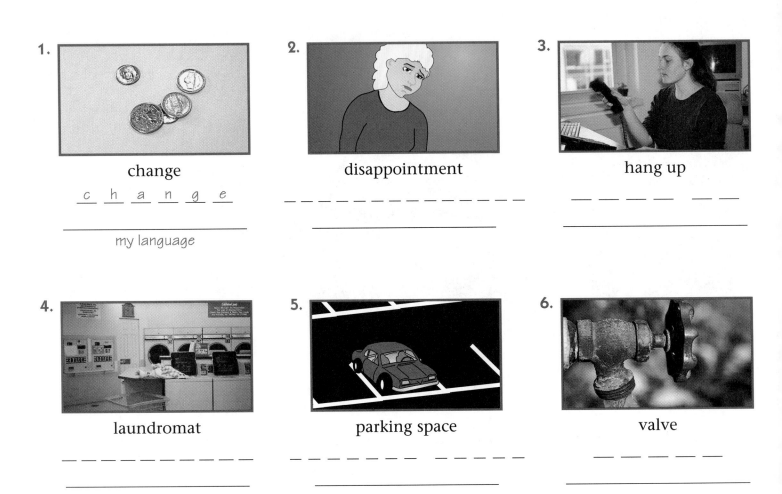

1. change

c h a n g e

_____

my language

2. disappointment

_ _ _ _ _ _ _ _ _ _ _ _ _ _

_____

3. hang up

_ _ _ _ _ _ _

_____

4. laundromat

_ _ _ _ _ _ _ _ _ _

_____

5. parking space

_ _ _ _ _ _ _ _ _ _ _ _

_____

6. valve

_ _ _ _ _

_____

Glossary

approve: admire, like. *Her parents do not approve of the way she dresses.*

go together: to go out with one person and no one else. *They went together for 10 years before they married.*

prejudice: having an opinion, good or bad, based on feelings not fact. *She is prejudiced against men with long hair.*

rude: not polite, behaving badly. *It was rude to walk away when she was talking.*

trust: believe in. *I trust him to keep a secret.*

upset: troubled and unhappy. *He is upset because he can not find a job.*

16 The Bottom Line

The stove at Crossroads Café does not work well. Mr. Brashov needs money to buy a new stove. He wants to borrow money from his bank. The banker visits the café.

What happens when the banker visits?

Who's in This Story?

Victor Brashov
the café owner

Mr. Lewis Littleton
vice president of a bank

Jess
a regular customer

Harry
president of a senior
citizens group

Rosa
the cook

Katherine
the waitress

Jamal
the handyman

Henry
the busboy

7

8

9

10

11

12

13

✓ **Check Yourself**

1. Why isn't Jess at the café every day?
   a. He doesn't like to go out in bad weather.
   b. He plays chess at a senior citizens center.

2. Why doesn't Mr. Brashov buy a new stove?
   a. He doesn't want to.
   b. He doesn't have the money.

14

15

16

17

18

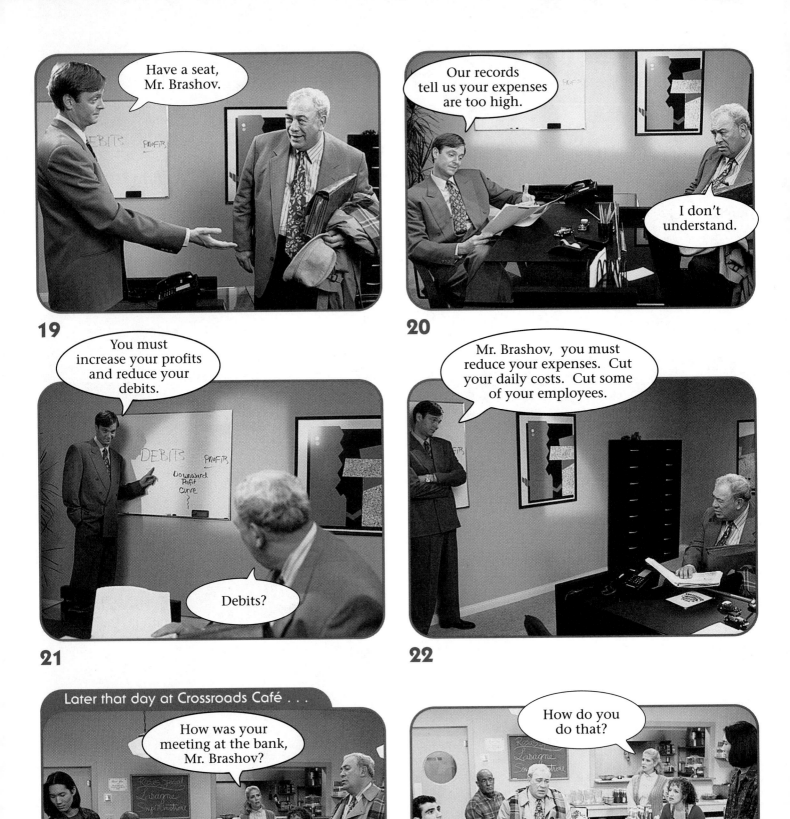

Crossroads Café   Photo Stories B

25

26

27

28

They start to make a flyer.

29

✓ Check Yourself

3. What does the banker tell Mr. Brashov?
   a. He must reduce his expenses.
   b. He must reduce his profit.

4. How do the workers plan to help Mr. Brashov?
   a. They will help Mr. Brashov cut his expenses.
   b. They will help Mr. Brashov attract more customers.

30

31

The next day at Crossroads Café . . .

Henry! Look what your flyers did.

My flyers didn't do that, Mr. Brashov. I slept late this morning. I didn't deliver them.

32

Victor, say hello to Harry. Harry is the president of our senior citizens group.

Jess told me about your problem. I talked the group into coming here for their morning coffee break.

33

I'm very happy to have you here. Please make yourself comfortable.

I will. Jess says you serve a great cup of coffee.

34

Your banker will be happy when he sees all these people.

35

A short time later . . .

This is horrible. Nobody is ordering anything.

36

Jess, your idea is not working.

37 The café is full, but nobody is eating.

38 Mr. Littleton arrives.

Welcome to Crossroads Café.

39 Please, sit. What can I get you?

Oh . . . a cup of coffee will be fine.

40 Here you are.

Mr. Brashov, no one is eating.

41 This is not the answer to your problems, Mr. Brashov. You have to make some big changes before it's too late.

42

✓ **Check Yourself**

5. Why does the café have many customers?

   a. because of Henry's flyers

   b. because of Jess's friends

6. Why isn't the banker happy?

   a. because the customers aren't eating

   b. because he doesn't like old people

43 Mr. Littleton leaves.

What did he mean by make some big changes?

I have to reduce my expenses.

44 Mr. Brashov exits to the back and Jamal enters.

What's wrong?

Mr. Brashov has to cut his expenses. Someone is going to lose his job.

Or **her** job.

45 A few days later . . .

Close the door, Henry. It's freezing in here.

I wanted to clear the snow off the sidewalk.

46

You're just worried that Mr. Brashov will fire you.

47

I think Mr. Brashov will fire me. He can cook.

What about Jamal?

48

Where **is** Jamal?

Maybe he's sick.

No. I called his home. Jihan thought he was here at work.

49

50

51

52

53

54

55

56

57

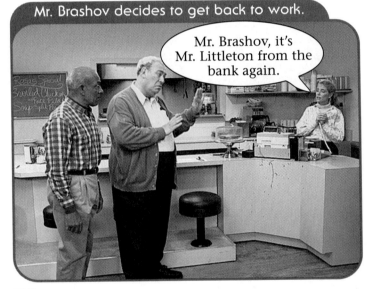

58

59

60

61

62

63

64

65

66

67

They're going to be here every week from now on.

Who are you?

68

A friend.

We're talking to other organizations about having their meetings here also.

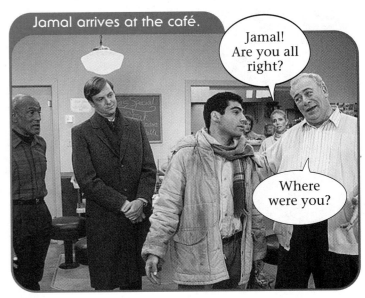

69

That's a good idea. Continue the good work. Maybe we can give you that loan.

70

Jamal arrives at the café.

Jamal! Are you all right?

Where were you?

71

I was looking for this part for the stove. Now I can fix it.

That is wonderful news. Well, Mr. Littleton, now I will not need that loan.

72

✓ **Check Yourself**

9. Why does the banker come back?
   a. because the café has lots of customers
   b. because Mr. Brashov didn't return his phone calls

10. What does Jamal find?
    a. a new job
    b. a part for the stove

Tell the Story

Match the picture with the sentence. Then tell the story to someone.

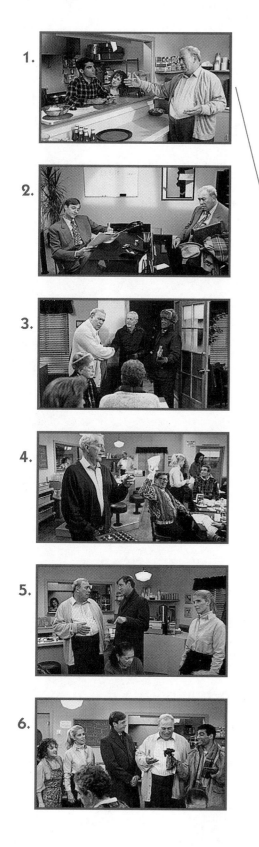

a. The banker tells Mr. Brashov he has to make some changes.

b. Jess brings Harry and the senior citizens to the café.

c. Mr. Brashov has a meeting at the bank.

d. Jamal finds the part for the stove, so Mr. Brashov doesn't need the loan.

e. Mr. Brashov, Rosa, and Jamal worry about the stove.

f. The senior citizens play bingo and eat lunch.

Search

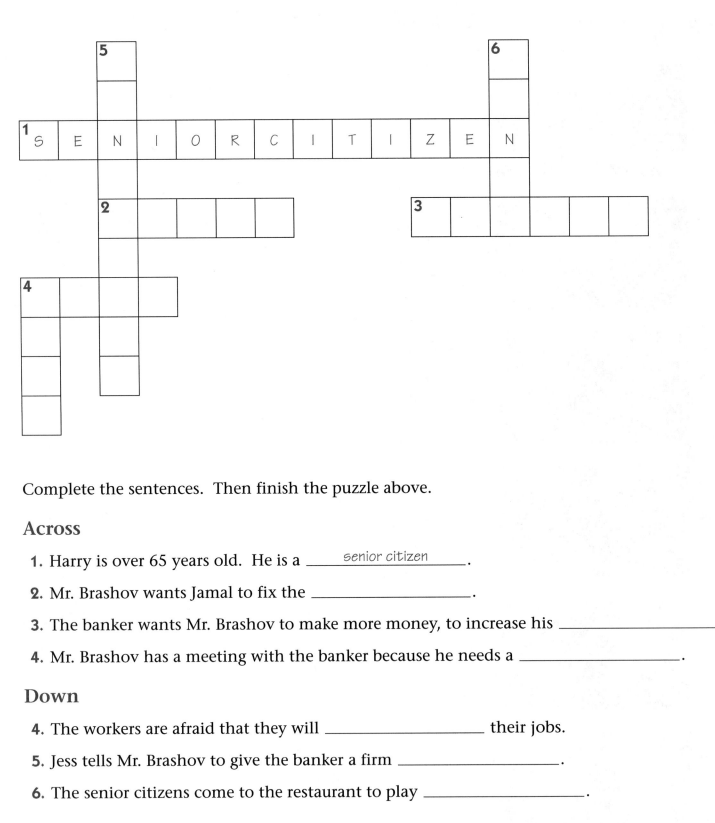

Complete the sentences. Then finish the puzzle above.

Across

1. Harry is over 65 years old. He is a _____senior citizen_____.

2. Mr. Brashov wants Jamal to fix the _____.

3. The banker wants Mr. Brashov to make more money, to increase his _____.

4. Mr. Brashov has a meeting with the banker because he needs a _____.

Down

4. The workers are afraid that they will _____ their jobs.

5. Jess tells Mr. Brashov to give the banker a firm _____.

6. The senior citizens come to the restaurant to play _____.

Build Your Vocabulary

The Banker's Office

Read the words in the list. Find the numbers in the picture.

1. white board
2. desk
3. telephone
4. pencil holder
5. paper organizer
6. hat
7. overcoat
8. scarf
9. folder

Complete the sentences. Use the words from the picture.

1. Mr. Brashov's _____scarf (8)_____ is black, gray, brown, and white.

2. Mr. Brashov is not wearing his _____. He is holding it in his hand.

3. I think it is cold outside, because Mr. Brashov has an _____.

4. The _____ on Mr. Littleton's desk has five pencils in it.

5. Mr. Littleton has a black _____. It is on the left side of his desk.

6. Mr. Littleton's _____, on the right side of his desk, doesn't have many papers in it.

7. Mr. Littleton is sitting behind his _____.

8. A _____ with some writing is on the wall.

9. Mr. Brashov is carrying his papers in a brown cardboard _____.

Picture Dictionary

Study the picture and the English word. Copy the word. Then you may write the word in your language.

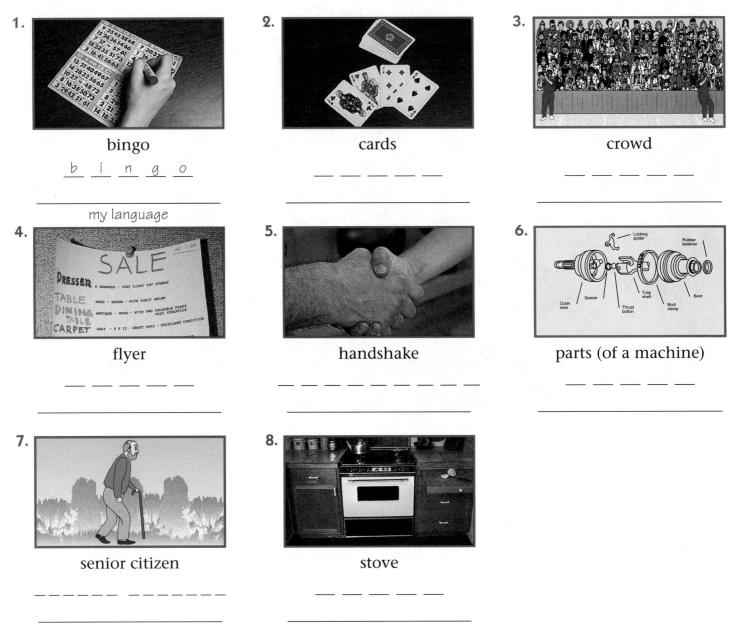

1. bingo

b i n g o

_____
my language

2. cards

_ _ _ _ _

_____

3. crowd

_ _ _ _ _

_____

4. flyer

_ _ _ _ _

_____

5. handshake

_____

_____

6. parts (of a machine)

_ _ _ _ _

_____

7. senior citizen

_ _ _ _ _ _ _ _ _ _ _ _ _

_____

8. stove

_ _ _ _ _

_____

Glossary

attract: make interested, appeal to. *She likes to save money, so sales attract her.*

debit: money owed, not yet paid. *His credit is good because he never has any debits.*

fire: dismiss from a job. *The company fired him because he was always late for work.*

loan: money that someone gives you and you need to pay back. *He never paid back the $300 loan, so we are no longer friends.*

profit: money above expenses. *The cost of the book is $12. They sell it for $20. They make an $8 profit.*

reduce: make or use less. *I want to reduce the amount of meat I eat.*

17 United We Stand

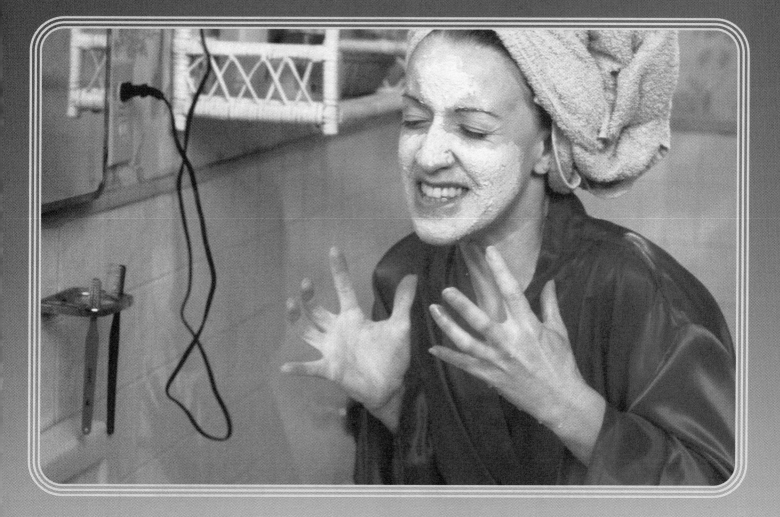

Rosa has a problem with her apartment.
The landlord doesn't answer her phone calls.
The Crossroads Café employees help her.

What do they do about the problem?

Who's in This Story?

Rosa
the cook

Jamal
the handyman

the manager of Rosa's
apartment building

Dr. Steven Martínez
an owner of Rosa's
apartment building

Henry
the busboy and a
high school student

Michael McAllister
a TV newscaster

Victor Brashov
the café owner

Katherine
the waitress

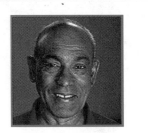

Jess
a regular customer

1

3

5

2

4

6

I'm sorry I'm late.

7

I didn't have any water in my apartment.

Hurry and get started.

8

If you have a plumbing problem, I can help.

Let me give the landlord one more call.

9

It's the answering machine again.

10

Jamal, would you take a look?

I'll come over after work.

11

✓ Check Yourself

1. Why is Rosa late?
   a. Her bus ran out of gas.
   b. Her apartment had no water.

2. Who can help with the plumbing?
   a. Jamal
   b. Jess

12

19

20

21

22

23

24

25

✓ **Check Yourself**

3. Who is Rosa writing a letter to?

   a. a tenant

   b. her landlord

4. What does Katherine think of Rosa's letter?

   a. It is too nice.

   b. It is not nice enough.

26

27

28

29

30

31 In the utility room, Rosa is changing her letter.

I know you are a busy man, but my brother is a lawyer and he says . . .

32

Hi Jamal. Where have you been?

I was doing errands.

33 Henry enters with his video camera.

Michael McAllister is going to see my video.

Michael McAllister, the newscaster?

Yes, he teaches my class.

34 Henry returns to the dining room.

This probably won't help your back, but it might cheer you up.

Thank you, Katherine.

35

Is there a Rosa Rivera here?

Henry, please stop the camera and go get Rosa.

Sure, Mr. Brashov.

36

I'm Rosa Rivera.

I'm from the property management company. We don't have your rent check yet.

37

38

39

40

41

42

✓ **Check Yourself**

5. Who comes to the café to see Rosa?

   a. a man who wants her rent

   b. a man who can fix pipes

6. What does Jess tell Rosa to do about the problems at her apartment?

   a. refuse to pay her rent

   b. organize the tenants

43

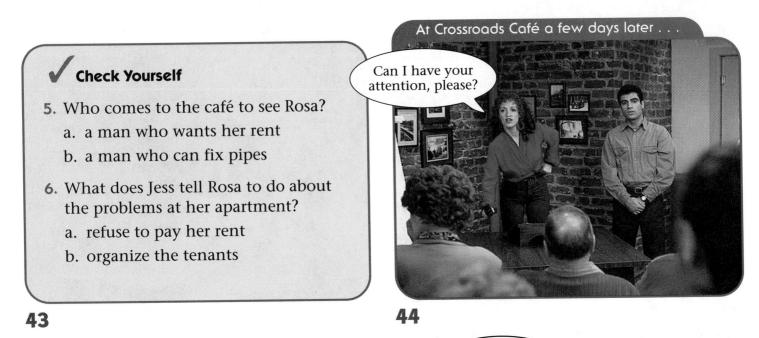

At Crossroads Café a few days later . . .

Can I have your attention, please?

44

Henry, where were you? You were going to help us get ready.

I had to stay at school. I need to talk to Rosa before she starts.

45

Why? What is so important?

I showed Michael McAllister my video project. He is coming here.

46

Rosa, can I talk with you?

I'll talk to you after the meeting. O.K.?

47

We'd like to start the meeting. Everybody please sit down.

48

49

We all want to improve our building. That's why we're here. Does anyone have any ideas?

50

Let's take pictures of all the problems.

51

I am Dr. Martínez. I own property in the area. I want to help.

52

We need basic services and safe conditions.

53

No water, no rent!

No water, no rent!

54

✓ **Check Yourself**

7. What does Henry want to tell Rosa?

   a. He is sorry he didn't help get ready.

   b. His teacher, a newscaster, is coming to the meeting.

8. Who is Dr. Martínez?

   a. a property owner

   b. a tenant

55

Early the next afternoon at Crossroads Café . . .

Quick, turn on Channel 8.

56

I still can't believe Michael McAllister came to the meeting.

When he saw my video, he said it would make a great story.

57

In local news, at Crossroads Café last night . . .

58

The TV shows the meeting at Crossroads Café.

DOWN WITH SLUMLORDS

59

Hey. That's my arm. I'm on TV!

Quiet, Henry. Here's that guy who owns property.

60

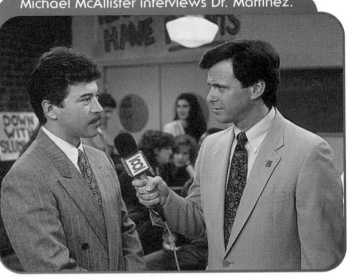

Michael McAllister interviews Dr. Martínez.

61

62

63

64

65

66

67

68

69

70

71

72

✓ **Check Yourself**

9. What is Michael McAllister's evening news program about?
   a. the tenants' meeting
   b. Henry's video project

10. Why does Mr. Martínez come to the café?
    a. to ask Rosa to stop talking about the problems
    b. to ask Rosa to talk about the problems with his partners

Tell the Story

Match the picture with the sentence. Then tell the story to someone.

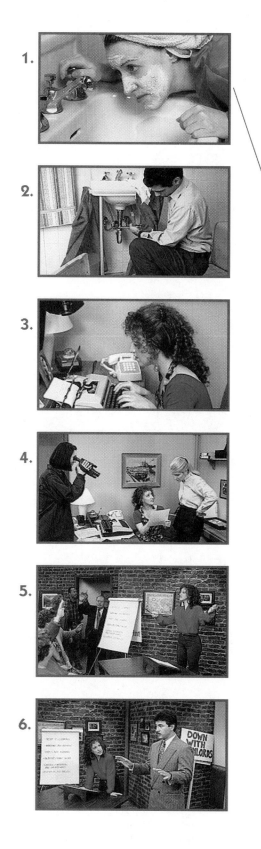

1.

2.

3.

4.

5.

6.

a. Rosa organizes a tenants' meeting.

b. Katherine helps Rosa write her letter.

c. One of the owners comes to the meeting.

d. Rosa has a water problem.

e. Rosa writes a letter to her landlord.

f. Jamal fixes the pipes.

Search

Unscramble the letters. Complete each sentence.

1. Jess hurt his _____back_____. (a c b k)

2. Jess told Rosa to organize the _____. (s n a n t e t)

3. Henry uses a _____ for his school project. (v e d o i a m c r a e)

4. Rosa wrote a _____ to her landlord. (e t r t l e)

5. Dr. Martinez invites Rosa to a _____. (n e m t e g i)

6. Jamal fixes Rosa's _____. (p e i p s)

7. Dr. Martinez is one of the _____. (w o r n e s)

8. Rosa wanted to wash her _____. (c e f a)

Now find each word below. When you find a word, circle it.

```
B  A  C  K  X  R  T  A  C  I  C  I  P
G  P  U  L  E  T  T  E  R  H  Z  A  I
I  A  M  E  E  T  I  N  G  E  K  N  P
P  T  Y  A  E  C  O  C  R  K  F  L  E
V  I  D  E  O  C  A  M  E  R  A  L  S
T  S  Z  O  W  N  E  R  S  X  C  P  U
J  T  E  N  A  N  T  S  L  I  E  Q  P
```

Build Your Vocabulary

Rosa's Bathroom

Read the words in the list. Find the numbers in the picture.

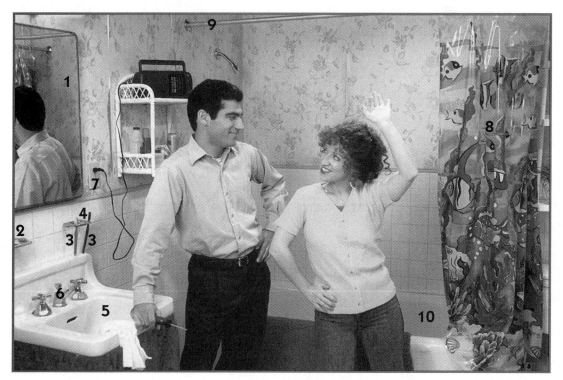

1. mirror
2. soap dish
3. toothbrushes
4. toothbrush holder
5. sink
6. faucet
7. outlet
8. shower curtain
9. shower rod
10. bathtub

Complete the sentences. Use the words from the picture.

1. Jamal has his hand on the _____ sink (5) _____.

2. The radio is plugged into the _____.

3. They are standing in front of the _____.

4. You can see Jamal's back in the _____.

5. The _____ has two handles, one for hot water and one for cold water.

6. The _____ for holding soap is above the sink.

7. There are two _____. One is pink and one is blue.

8. There are two toothbrushes in the _____.

9. The tub has a colorful _____ so water won't get on the floor.

10. The shower curtain is hanging from a _____.

Picture Dictionary

Study the picture and the English word. Copy the word. Then you may write the word in your language.

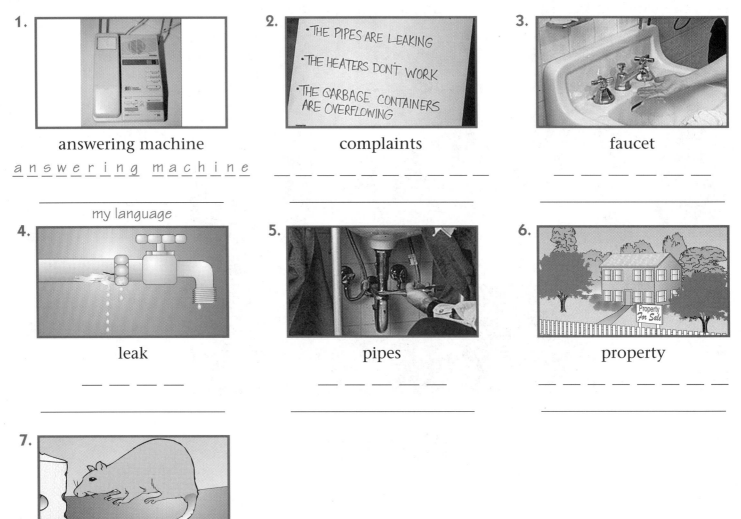

1. answering machine

a n s w e r i n g   m a c h i n e

_____

my language

2. complaints

• THE PIPES ARE LEAKING

• THE HEATERS DON'T WORK

• THE GARBAGE CONTAINERS ARE OVERFLOWING

_____

_____

3. faucet

_____

4. leak

_____

5. pipes

_____

_____

6. property

Property For Sale

_____

_____

7. rat

_____

Glossary

aggressive: strong; pushy. *I don't like to buy cars because the salespeople are so aggressive.*

apologize: to say you are sorry for doing something wrong. *My son apologized for breaking his friend's toy.*

documentary: a film or television program about facts or history. *My favorite television programs are documentaries about wild animals.*

landlord: owner of building that is rented to others. *The landlord lives in another town so he doesn't take good care of the building.*

plumbing: pipes, faucets, and fixtures such as bathtub, toilet, and sink. *Plumbing problems can cause high water bills.*

tenant: a person who rents space to live or work. *The tenants wrote a letter about the garbage and water service.*

18 Opportunity Knocks

Jamal accepts a job as an engineer for a construction firm. He thinks it is a good opportunity. Then he begins to think about the choice he made.

What happens to Jamal at his new job?

Who's in This Story?

Jamal
the café handyman

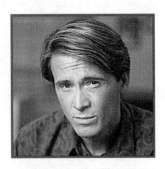

Rich Marshall
the construction company
owner

Joe Cassidy
a project manager

Bobby
a construction worker

Victor Brashov
the café owner

Henry
the busboy and
delivery person

Katherine
the waitress

Rosa
the cook

Jess
a regular customer

13

14

15

16

✓ Check Yourself

1. What does Mr. Brashov bring into the café?
   a. new furniture
   b. a jukebox

2. Who gives Jamal a business card?
   a. the delivery man
   b. a customer

17

18

25

✓ **Check Yourself**

3. Why does Mr. Marshall want to talk to Jamal?
   a. because he needs an engineer
   b. because he wants Jamal to fix something

4. Where does Jamal go to see Mr. Marshall?
   a. to the café
   b. to the construction site

26

27

28

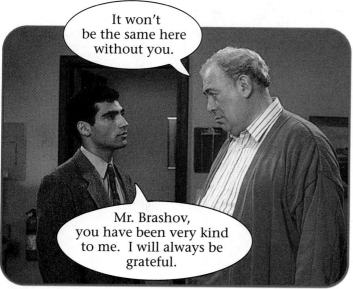

29

30

31

Jamal is working at his new job.

Ahh . . . Jihan, I just spilled coffee all over the desk!

32

This computer disk is covered with coffee. I hope these files are O.K.

33

I'm trying the disk now. Wait a second.

34

Oh good, everything looks O.K.

35

Jamal sees something strange on the computer screen.

36

37

38

39

40

41

42

49

No one is going to get hurt. Just sign the forms!

Mr. Marshall gives Jamal the forms and an envelope.

50

Jamal opens the envelope.

51

Jamal wants to talk to someone about Mr. Marshall.

I would like the number of the Department of Building and Safety.

52

✓ Check Yourself

7. What does Jamal find out about his boss?
   a. that he makes a lot of money
   b. that he uses old building materials

8. Why does Mr. Marshall give Jamal an envelope of money?
   a. so Jamal can buy some new materials
   b. so Jamal will not talk about the problems he sees

53

A few days later Mr. Brashov has interviews for the handyman job.

Thank you for coming in. I will let you know.

Thanks.

54

55

56

57

58

59

60

✓ Check Yourself

9. What is Mr. Brashov doing?

   a. He is talking to people about the handyman job.

   b. He is ordering supplies.

10. Who does Mr. Brashov hire as the handyman?

    a. Joe Cassidy

    b. Jamal

Tell the Story

Put the pictures and sentences in order. Number 1 to 6. Then tell the story to someone.

___ a.

Jamal is a handyman again.

___ b.

Mr. Marshall is angry at Jamal.

__1__ c.

A customer talks on a phone
in the café.

___ d.

Mr. Marshall takes Jamal to
a worksite.

___ e.

Jamal sees something strange
on the computer.

___ f.

Jamal makes a telephone call
about his boss.

Search

For each sentence in the box, write the number in a circle.

1. He likes his boss.

2. He looks at building materials.

3. He wears a tool belt at work.

4. He is offered money to do something wrong.

5. He wears a hard hat at work.

6. He makes many repairs.

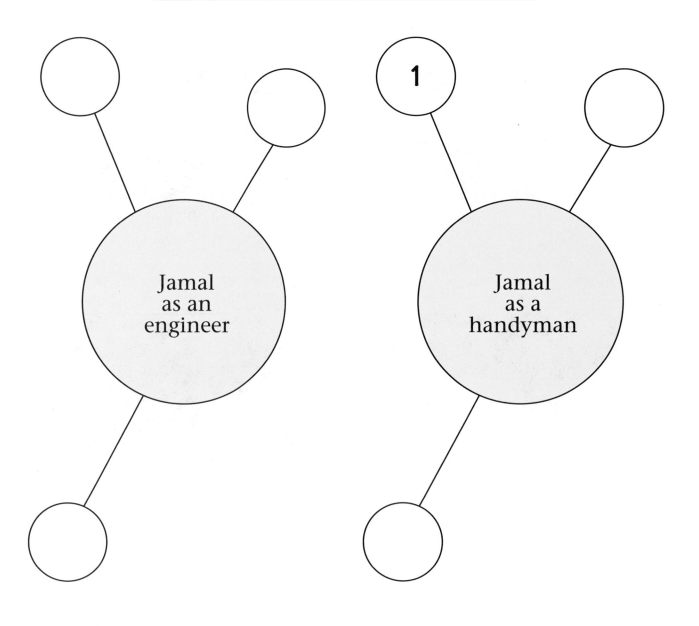

Jamal as an engineer

Jamal as a handyman

Build Your Vocabulary

Construction Site

Read the words in the list. Find the numbers in the picture.

1. hard hat
2. ladder
3. beams
4. vest
5. work boots
6. building plans
7. board

Complete the sentences. Use the words from the picture.

1. Two of the workers look at the ___building plans (6)___ .

2. The _____ hold up the weight of the building.

3. One of the workers is wearing a _____ over his shirt.

4. To do work in high places, the workers need to stand on a _____ .

5. The construction workers are wearing _____ to protect their feet.

6. Everybody at a construction site must wear a _____ for safety.

7. The worker is standing on top of a _____ .

Picture Dictionary

Study the picture and the English word. Copy the word. Then you may write the word in your language.

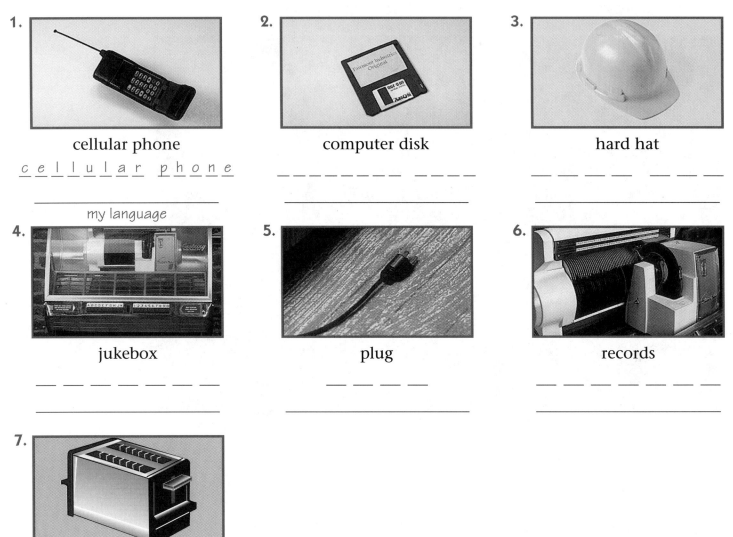

1.
cellular phone

_c e l l u l a r_ _p h o n e_

_____
my language

2.
computer disk

_ _ _ _ _ _ _ _ _ _ _ _

_____

3.
hard hat

_ _ _ _ _ _ _

_____

4.
jukebox

_ _ _ _ _ _ _

_____

5.
plug

_ _ _ _

_____

6.
records

_ _ _ _ _ _ _

_____

7.
toaster

_ _ _ _ _ _ _

_____

Glossary

accusation: a charge of crime or doing something wrong. *The workers made accusations against the owner for not paying overtime.*

deadline: a time or date by which something must be finished. *The teacher changed the deadline of the science report because the student was sick.*

engineer: a person trained in math and science who plans the building of machines, roads or bridges. *She studied very hard at school to become an engineer.*

file: a place to hold information. *The medical secretary needs another cabinet to hold all of the doctors' files.*

second-hand: used by someone else before. *He has to buy a second-hand car because he does not have the money for a new one.*

signature: a person's name that is written by the person himself/herself. *The writer put her signature on the first page of her new book.*

19 The People's Choice

Mr. Brashov and Jess have problems with city services. Jess decides to run for office.

What happens to Jess?

Who's in This Story?

Jess Washington
a regular customer
at the café

Carol Washington
Jess's wife

Dan Miller
a business man who works
for Andrew Comstock

Andrew Comstock
a real estate developer

Jamal
the handyman

Hassan
Jamal's cousin
visiting from Egypt

Victor Brashov
the café owner

Rosa
the cook

Katherine
the waitress

Henry
the busboy

7 Jamal arrives at work.

Did you see my cousin? I told him to wait in front of the café.

8 The man returns to the restaurant.

Hassan, what are you doing with those construction barriers?

They were blocking traffic.

9 Hassan, meet Mr. Brashov, Rosa, and Katherine.

Hello.

10

✓ **Check Yourself**

1. Why is Mr. Brashov unhappy?
   a. because of the construction barriers
   b. because of Hassan's visit

2. Who is Hassan?
   a. a construction worker
   b. Jamal's cousin

11 Later that same morning Jess arrives at the café.

What's this?

My water bill. Look at it.

12

$30,000 for one month of water? This is a mistake.

13

14

15

16

17

18

That night at Jess's house . . .

Some of the people at Crossroads Café had a crazy idea.

What was their idea?

19

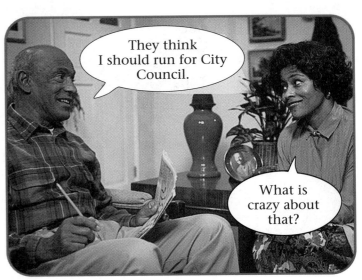

They think I should run for City Council.

What is crazy about that?

20

Politicians promise to do everything, but they do nothing. You can be the people's choice.

The people's choice. I like that.

21

✓ **Check Yourself**

3. Why is Jess unhappy with the city?
   a. because of his water bill
   b. because of the traffic

4. Who do the café employees want to run for city council?
   a. Mr. Brashov
   b. Jess

22

Several days later at Crossroads Café while the café is closed . . .

23

Everyone helps Jess with the campaign.

WASHINGTON FOR CITY COUNCIL

24

25

26

27

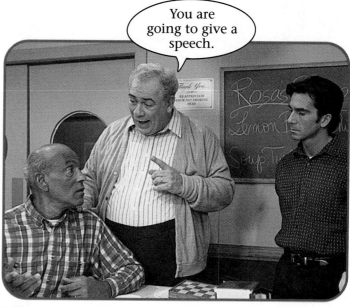

28

29

30

31

32

Two days later at Crossroads Café the man returns.

33

Jess prepares for his speech.

34

Jess begins to make a speech.

35

36

The people clap after Jess's speech.

37

Jess shakes hands.

38

Nice to see you again.

Good to see you again, too.

39

I want you to meet someone. Jess Washington, Andrew Comstock.

How do you do, Mr. Comstock.

Call me Andy.

40

I want to help you win. I think you will make an excellent councilman.

Thank you.

41

✓ **Check Yourself**

5. Why does Mr. Comstock come to the café?

   a. to taste Rosa's food

   b. to listen to Jess

6. What does Mr. Comstock decide to do?

   a. help Jess win the election

   b. buy the café from Mr. Brashov

42

43 Several days later at Crossroads Café . . .

Mr. Brashov, look who's here.

44 Jess, you look different.

My advisors think I need to change my image.

45 Why are you sitting here and not at the counter?

I have a meeting to discuss issues.

46 Issues like that telephone hot line?

No, my advisors don't think it's important.

47 A day or two later Jess campaigns from door to door.

48 The campaign team works.

49

50

51

52

53

54

55

56

57

58

59

60

61

62

63

64

65

66

67

Election night, a few nights later . . .

O.K. everybody. This is it.

68

Washington 18,422.

69

Tom Johansen is the winner.

70

I'm sorry, Jess.

As far as I'm concerned, you did win.

71

✓ **Check Yourself**

9. Why does Jess throw away his speech and take off his toupee?

   a. He doesn't feel comfortable.

   b. Comstock and Miller don't like them.

10. Does Jess win the election?

   a. Yes, he wins it.

   b. No, he loses it.

72

Tell the Story

Put the pictures and sentences in order. Number 1 to 8. Then tell the story to someone.

____ a.

Jess loses the election, but
Carol is happy.

____ b.

The Crossroads Café workers
help with Jess's campaign.

____ c.

Dan Miller introduces Jess
to Andy Comstock.

<u>1</u> d.

Jess has a problem with
his water bill.

____ e.

Jess decides he doesn't like
the changes either.

____ f.

Carol wants Jess to run for
City Council.

____ g.

Miller and Comstock change the
way Jess looks and thinks.

____ h.

Carol doesn't like the changes.

Search

For each sentence in the box, write the number in a circle.

> 1. The city needs a telephone hotline.
>
> 2. A telephone hotline is not an issue.
>
> 3. People need answers about their bills.
>
> 4. Parking lots are more important than buildings.
>
> 5. He changes his looks.
>
> 6. He tears up his speech and takes off his toupee.
>
> 7. Politicians need to work for the people.

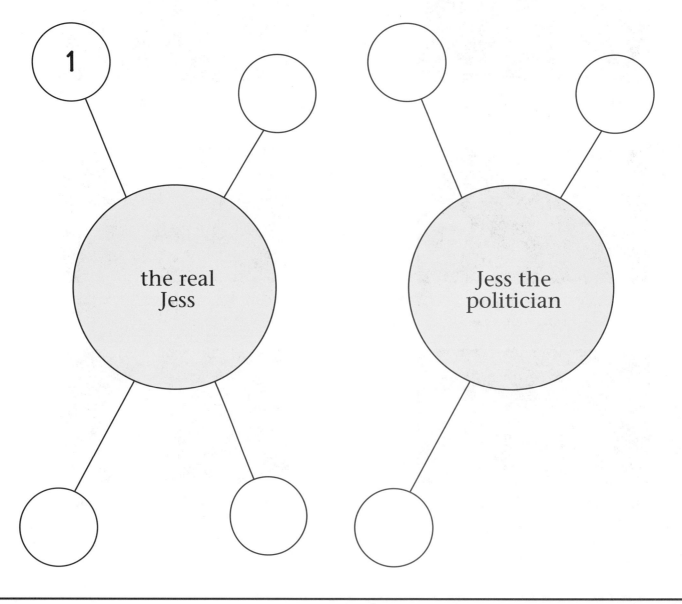

Build Your Vocabulary

Jess's Campaign

Read the words in the list. Find the numbers in the picture.

1. flag
2. balloons
3. banner
4. campaign buttons
5. bumper sticker
6. poster
7. podium

Complete the sentences. Use the words from the picture.

1. Jess is standing at a _____podium (7)_____ .

2. A campaign _____ is behind him.

3. _____ are to his left.

4. A red, white, and blue _____ is beside the door to the kitchen.

5. The _____ on the wall has a picture of Jess.

6. A woman in the front row is holding a _____ .

7. The men are wearing _____ on their jackets.

Picture Dictionary

Study the picture and the English word. Copy the word. Then you may write the word in your language.

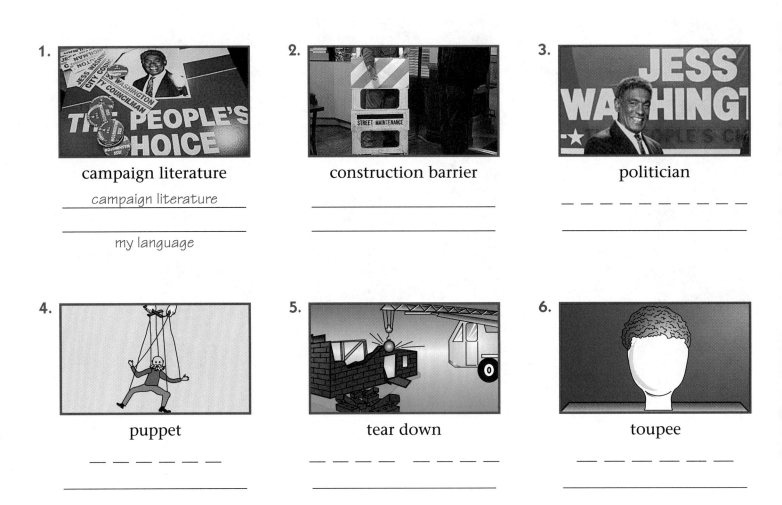

1. campaign literature

   campaign literature

   my language

2. construction barrier

3. politician

4. puppet

5. tear down

6. toupee

Glossary

advisor: a person who gives advice. *When students have trouble with their grades, they should see their advisor.*

campaign: working together for a goal. *The goal for the school's money raising campaign is one million dollars.*

city council: people elected to make laws and decisions for a city. *City council meetings are open to the public.*

election: when people vote for or against something or someone. *Who did you vote for in the last election?*

hot line: a telephone line for emergencies. *After the earthquake, the city started a hotline for people to call for help.*

voter survey: questions to get the opinions of voters. *Before a national election, there are voter surveys every week.*

Rosa is taking a business class. Her teacher
is having a party for some businessmen. He
needs a translator. He asks Rosa.

What happens?

Who's in This Story?

Rosa Rivera
the café cook

Andrew Collins
Rosa's teacher

Libby Flanders
Andrew's friend

Victor Brashov
the café owner

Mr. Shuster
the café landlord

Stuart Shuster
Mr. Shuster's
10-year-old son

Ricardo
a businessman
from South America

Katherine
the waitress

Bill
Katherine's friend

Henry
the busboy

Jamal
the handyman

7

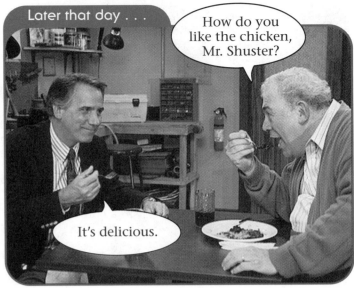

8

9

10

11

12

13

14

15

16

17

18

✓ **Check Yourself**

1. Why does Mr. Brashov want Rosa to cook something special?
   a. because his landlord is coming for lunch
   b. because Bill is coming to see Katherine

2. Why does Rosa's teacher come to the café?
   a. to ask her to go out with him
   b. to ask her to translate for him

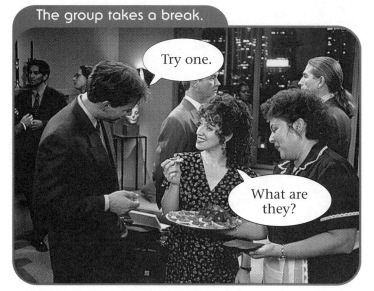

25

The group takes a break.

Try one.

What are they?

26

Foie gras.

Ah, goose liver. Very fancy.

27

Rosa doesn't like the *foie gras.* The maid helps her.

28

Miss Rivera is a very good translator.

Rosa is a student in the business class I'm teaching. Rosa, Max is one of my investors.

29

A new guest arrives.

Andrew, this is quite a party. Are you going to introduce me to your new friend?

This is Rosa Rivera.

I'm Libby Flanders.

Hello. It's nice to meet you.

30

What do you think the painting is about?

Maybe I should ask my ten-year-old sister. She always draws like this.

31

Andrew moves away to talk to one of the businessmen.

You are not right for Andrew. He likes expensive art, antiques, fine wines.

32

Rosa speaks to the maid in Spanish, and Libby comments.

You won't become a part of Andrew's world by talking with the help.

33

✓ **Check Yourself**

3. What does Mr. Shuster plan to do with his son?
   a. take him to the library
   b. take him to a ball game

4. What does Libby tell Rosa?
   a. She is right for Andrew because she is a good translator.
   b. She is not right for Andrew because he likes expensive art, antiques, and fine wine.

34

The following morning before the café opens . . .

35

Why are you interested in modern art?

I want to talk about it with Andrew when we go out.

36

I thought you were just translating for him.

Well, I was and . . . he asked me out.

Rosa talks in Spanish with Ricardo about a wine he is drinking.

Estos vinos son del '89 de las regiones de Burgundy y de Bordeaux.

You know a lot about wine.

43

Ricardo speaks to Rosa in Spanish, and Rosa translates for Andrew.

Dígale a señor Collins que le debería aumentar su sueldo.

What did he say?

He said you should give me a raise.

44

I didn't tell him that I don't work for you.

Well, maybe that's something we should talk about.

45

✓ **Check Yourself**

5. Why is Rosa studying art, music, and wine?
   a. She thinks they are important for her job.
   b. She wants to be able to talk with Andrew.

6. What does Stuart want to do?
   a. have a milkshake and a piece of pie
   b. look at Mr. Brashov's accounts

46

Early the next afternoon at Crossroads Café . . .

You should wear gloves.

I know when there is a safety problem.

47

Jamal angrily leaves his work.

Excuse me!

48

55

He plays very well.

Wait outside Stuart. I'll be right out.

It's Stu. I don't want to be called Stuart anymore.

56

Stu Shuster. I like the way that sounds.

57

Thank you.

You aren't angry?

No. You did in one day what I couldn't do in ten years.

58

✔ **Check Yourself**

7. What do Jamal and Henry do with Stuart?
   a. show him how to play soccer
   b. make him do their jobs

8. Why is Mr. Shuster happy?
   a. because Mr. Brashov helps Stuart write a good report
   b. because Jamal and Henry show Stuart how to play soccer

59

Night at Andrew's apartment . . .

Hi, Andrew. I came as soon as I could. What's going on?

60

I got the money for the restaurants.

That's great news.

61

62

63

64

65

66

67 — A few days later at Crossroads Café . . .

"You're still thinking about Andrew."

"No. I am thinking that I was foolish. I thought we were more than friends."

68

"Bill! What a nice surprise!"

"I took an early plane."

69

"So were you successful?"

"Look and see."

70

71

"Will you marry me?"

"Yes!"

72

✓ **Check Yourself**

9. What does Rosa do with Andrew's present?
   a. She gives it back to him.
   b. She drinks it.

10. Why does Bill give Katherine a ring?
    a. She collects rings.
    b. He wants to marry her.

Tell the Story

Match the picture with the sentence. Then tell the story to someone.

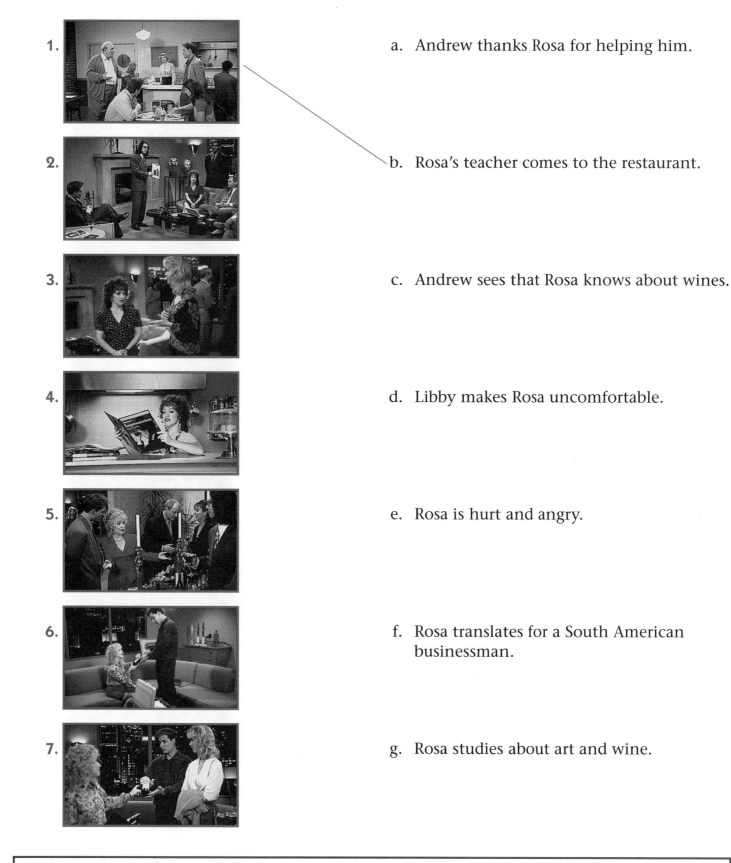

1.

2.

3.

4.

5.

6.

7.

a. Andrew thanks Rosa for helping him.

b. Rosa's teacher comes to the restaurant.

c. Andrew sees that Rosa knows about wines.

d. Libby makes Rosa uncomfortable.

e. Rosa is hurt and angry.

f. Rosa translates for a South American businessman.

g. Rosa studies about art and wine.

Search

For each sentence in the box, write the number in a circle.

> 1. Rosa hides the *foie gras* in a napkin.
>
> 2. Rosa explains wine to Ricardo.
>
> 3. Rosa speaks to the maid in English
>
> 4. Rosa speaks to the maid in Spanish.
>
> 5. Rosa says the painting looks like her 10-year-old sister's work.
>
> 6. Rosa explains a piece of modern art.

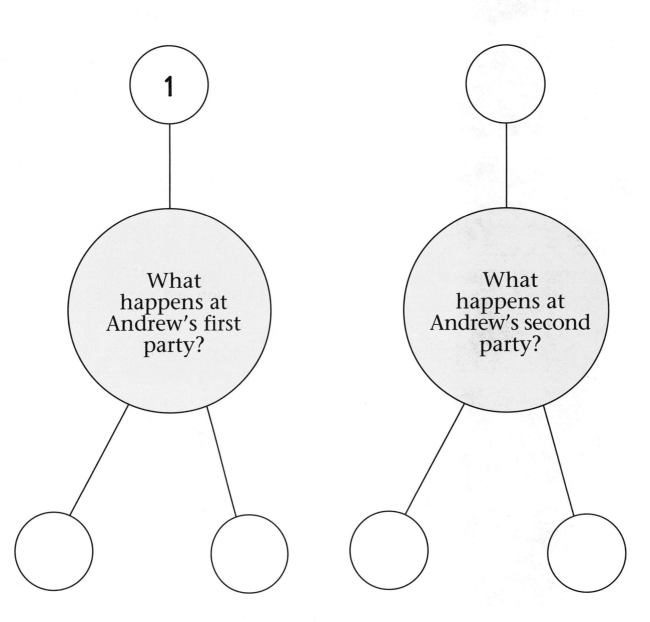

Build Your Vocabulary

Andrew's Party

Read the words in the list. Find the numbers in the picture.

1. paintings
2. buffet table
3. bottles of wine
4. glass of wine
5. trays
6. cheese
7. knife
8. bread

Complete the sentences. Use the words from the picture.

1. Food and drinks are on the _____buffet table (2)_____.

2. The food is on _____.

3. One tray has several kinds of _____.

4. The tray also has a _____ to cut the cheese.

5. The other tray has some slices of _____.

6. Several _____ are on the table, some opened and some unopened.

7. Each guest is holding a _____.

8. Two _____ are hanging on the wall.

Picture Dictionary

Study the picture and the English word. Copy the word. Then you may write the word in your language.

1.

RECORD ALL CHARGES THAT AFFECT YOUR ACCOUNT

accounts

a c c o u n t s

_____
my language

2.

antiques

— — — — — — — —

_____

3.

art

— — —

_____

4.

bear

— — — —

_____

5.

engagement ring

— — — — — — — — — — —

_____

6.

soccer

— — — — — —

_____

7.

South America

— — — — — — — — — — —

_____

8.

wine

— — — —

_____

Glossary

accountant: a person who prepares records about money. *They have an accountant prepare their taxes.*

collect: gather or save. *He collects stamps from different countries.*

investor: a person who gives money to a business in order to make money. *That company needs money, so it is looking for investors.*

landlord: owner of a building that is rented to others. *When a landlord's expenses increase, he increases the rent.*

translate: to change one language to another language. *I can't read this. Would you translate it for me?*

translator: a person who translates. *It is difficult to find translators for the Russian language.*

21 Walls and Bridges

Rosa's young friend María has trouble
attending school. María's teacher talks to
Rosa about the problem. Rosa helps María.

How does Rosa help María?

Who's in This Story?

Rosa
María's "big sister"
and the café cook

César Hernandez
María's father, a tailor
and café janitor

María Hernandez
César's daughter, a
high school student and
Rosa's "little sister"

Blanca Hernandez
María's mother
a seamstress

Chris Scanlon
María's teacher

Victor Brashov
the café owner

Jess
a regular customer

Jamal
the handyman

Katherine
the waitress

Henry
the busboy and
delivery person

1

2

3

4

5

6

7

8

9

10

11

12

13

14

15

16

17

18

The next day at the café . . .

Jamal, what are you doing?

I am fixing a stool. How is your studying coming?

Good.

19

Mr. Brashov, after so many years, why do you want to be a citizen now?

20

I made a promise to my wife. I said I'd do something for this country.

21

✔ **Check Yourself**

1. Why is Mr. Brashov studying?
   a. He wants to go back to school.
   b. He wants to pass his citizenship exam.

2. Why does Mrs. Scanlon go to the café?
   a. to talk to Rosa about María
   b. to get something to eat

22

A few nights later at the Hernandez tailor shop . . .

23

María comes into the front room.

Rosa, what are you doing here?

I need to have some skirts shortened.

24

25

26

27

28

29

30

31

The next day at the café . . .

I went to the shop yesterday. That man . . . oh, that man . . .

Rosa, calm down!

32

María's father . . . he says that María does not need to go to school.

That's terrible. What are you going to do?

33

Maybe it is better to do nothing.

But, María is my friend.

And Mr. Hernandez is her father.

34

María comes into the café.

María, are you back in school?

No. I just delivered a dress to a customer. I wanted to say hello.

35

There are problems at the shop. So now I have to help.

36

But what about high school?

I can't think about high school now.

37

It's for students who need to work. I go to school until noon. Then I work here in the afternoon.

I can't do that. My father needs me in the shop all day, not part-time.

38

Rosa and Mrs. Scanlon go to talk to Mr. Hernandez about María.

✓ **Check Yourself**

3. Why doesn't María go to school?
   a. She doesn't like school.
   b. She has to work in her father's shop.

4. Why is Rosa angry with Mr. Hernandez?
   a. He wants María to work instead of going to school.
   b. He doesn't take care of his family.

39

40

María can be in a work-study program. She can go to school in the morning and work here in the afternoon.

41

Mr. Hernandez starts to speak in English.

I told you. We need María here.

42

43

44

45

46

47

48

49

50

51

52

53

54

Several hours later Rosa helps Mr. Brashov.

55

Later, Jamal wakes up and asks Mr. Brashov some questions.

56

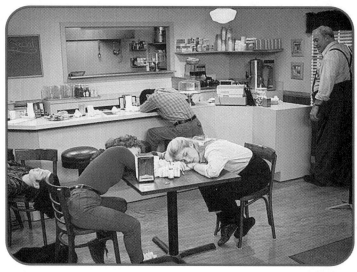

Who was Abraham Lincoln?

He was President during the Civil War.

57

58

The next morning Mr. Brashov is ready for his test.

Eva, I am going to take my citizenship test after all these years.

59

Wish me luck, Eva.

60

61

Mr. Brashov passed his test.

Good night, Mr. Brashov and congratulations again.

62

When do you become a citizen?

I don't know. But I passed the test with your help . . . that's the important thing.

63

I did it! I'm going to be a citizen!

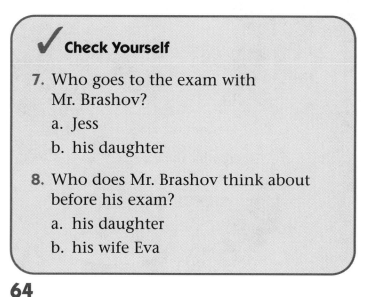

64

✓ **Check Yourself**

7. Who goes to the exam with Mr. Brashov?

a. Jess

b. his daughter

8. Who does Mr. Brashov think about before his exam?

a. his daughter

b. his wife Eva

65

Mr. Hernandez enters the café.

Hello, César. I passed my citizenship test today.

Congratulations! You must be proud.

66

But one thing is missing, my daughter.

Why isn't she here?

A few years ago we had a fight. Now we don't speak.

67

68

69

70

71

72

Tell the Story

Put the pictures and sentences in order. For each story, number 1 to 3. Then tell each story to someone.

Mr. Brashov's Story

____ a.

Mr. Brashov passes his citizenship test.

__1__ b.

Mr. Brashov tells Jamal about his exam.

____ c.

Everyone helps Mr. Brashov study for his exam.

María's Story

____ a.

Mr. Hernandez tells María he will talk with Mrs. Scanlon.

____ b.

Mrs. Scanlon and Rosa go to the shop to talk to María's father.

____ c.

Mrs. Scanlon talks to Rosa about María.

Search

Complete the sentences. Then finish the puzzle above.

Across

2. Mr. Brashov wants to become a _____*citizen*_____ .

5. Mr. Hernandez owns a _____ shop.

Down

1. Mrs. Hernandez does a lot of _____ at the shop.

3. Rosa and Mrs. Scanlon want María to finish _____ .

4. Jess helps Mr. Brashov study for his _____ .

Build Your Vocabulary

A Tailor Shop

Read the words in the list. Find the numbers in the picture.

1. clothes rack
2. fitting room
3. sewing machine
4. cloth
5. counter
6. cash register
7. spool of thread
8. lamp
9. mannequin

Complete the sentences. Use the words from the picture.

1. The worker puts money in the ___cash register (6)___ .

2. There are several pieces of _____ next to the sewing machine.

3. People try clothes on in the _____ .

4. The dresses are hanging on a _____ .

5. There is a dress on the _____ near the front window.

6. It is easy to make clothes when you have a _____ .

7. When it is dark near the sewing machine, the worker turns on the _____ .

8. There is a large, white _____ near the sewing machine.

9. The customers wait at the _____ .

Picture Dictionary

Study the picture and the English word. Copy the word. Then you may write the word in your language.

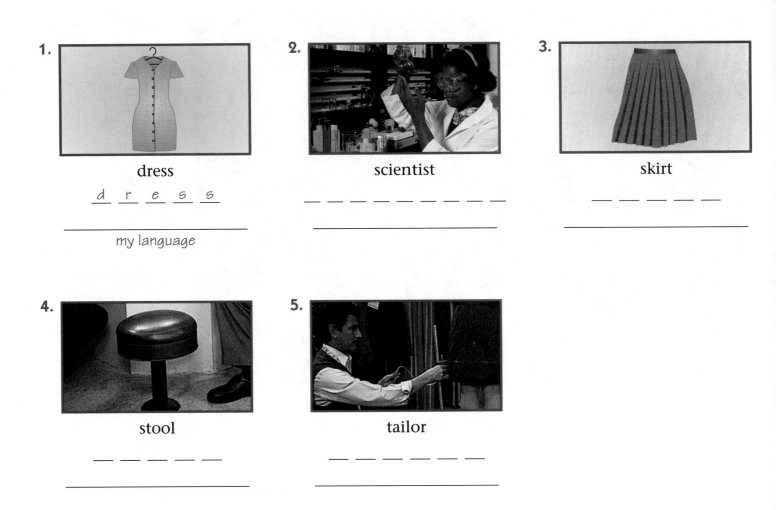

1. dress

d r e s s

_____
my language

2. scientist

_ _ _ _ _ _ _ _ _

_____

3. skirt

_ _ _ _ _

_____

4. stool

_ _ _ _ _

_____

5. tailor

_ _ _ _ _ _

_____

Glossary

award: a prize or honor given for doing something well. *The young man wins many awards because he plays baseball so well.*

citizen: a legal member of a country. *When people become citizens of the United States, they are allowed to vote.*

college: a place to continue studying after high school. *After she leaves high school, the young woman wants to go to college to study science.*

congratulations: an expression of praise or pleasure for something. *Many people say, "Congratulations!" to the mother and father when a baby is born.*

goulash: a stew of meat, vegetables, and spices. *One of Alice's favorite foods is goulash.*

part-time: taking up only part of a workday or work week. *The teenager has a part-time job at the restaurant; he works there only two nights a week.*

22 Helping Hands

One day a man surprises the workers at
the café. They learn about his problems
and try to help him.

What happens to the man?

Who's in This Story?

Frank
an unemployed
man

Marty
the post office
supervisor

Katherine
the café waitress

Jamal
the handyman

Jihan
Jamal's wife

Victor Brashov
the café owner

Jess
a regular customer

Henry
the busboy and
delivery person

Rosa
the cook

7

A few minutes later . . .

What do you want?

I need something to eat.

8

Katherine and Jess think the man is a robber.

Rosa? Make a turkey sandwich now!

9

One turkey sandwich right away.

10

Mr. Brashov, Jamal and Henry put their hands up, too.

What's going on here?

11

The workers think the man is taking a gun out of his pocket.

12

13

14

15

16

✓ **Check Yourself**

1. Who is going away?
   a. Jess
   b. Jamal

2. Why is the man in the café?
   a. He wants something to eat.
   b. He wants some money.

17

18

19

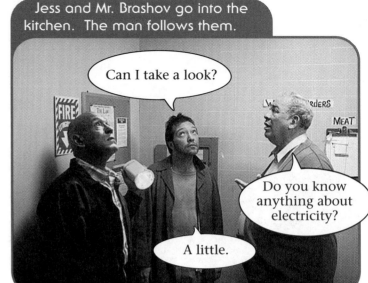

20

21

22

23

24

25

How did you know how to fix the lights?

It was part of my training. I'm an auto mechanic.

26

When was your last job?

A year and a half ago.

It is really hard to find a job. But don't give up.

27

I am so tired of people saying "no" to me. Only you have been kind. Thank you.

No. Thank **you** for fixing the lights.

28

✓ **Check Yourself**

3. Who fixes the lights?
   a. Frank
   b. Jess

4. What is Frank's job?
   a. He works as an auto mechanic.
   b. He has no job now.

That night at the hotel, Jamal and Azza wait for Jihan.

29

Hello? You found my luggage. Fantastic! When can I get it?

Several hours later Jihan returns from her meetings.

30

Hi! You're finally back.

I'm sorry that I'm late. The meeting was long.

31

32

33

34

35

36

37

✓ **Check Yourself**

5. Why is Jamal upset?
   a. His food at the hotel is not good.
   b. He doesn't have his luggage.

6. Who is the new handyman?
   a. Mr. Brashov
   b. Frank

38

The next day at the café . . .

Katherine tells me you hired that guy who was in here the other day.

His name is Frank. He is doing excellent work. I feel sorry for him. He has a hard life.

39

I can't believe how Mr. Brashov treats him.

There are a lot of people like Frank who don't have a job.

40

You have so many skills. Why don't you have a job?

I was laid off from the factory. I looked for other jobs. But I'm not good at interviews. I get nervous and I can't talk.

41

Jess comes back into the café.

My car won't start.

Wait a minute, Jess. Frank is a mechanic. He can look at it.

Yes. I would be happy to take a look.

42

43

Thank you. You saved me a lot of money.

No problem.

44

He is really good with cars. I think we can do something for him.

What?

My friend is the chief mechanic at the post office. Maybe he can help.

45

Jamal and Jihan return to the hotel from a party.

What's wrong, Jamal? Tell me.

I thought this trip was for all of us to enjoy. We never see you.

46

They start to argue.

What do you want? Do you want me to quit my job and stay home?

I don't know what I want.

47

✔ **Check Yourself**

7. How does Frank help Jess?

   a. He fixes his car.

   b. He gives him a ride.

8. What does Jamal want Jihan to do?

   a. spend more time on her job

   b. spend more time with him and the baby

48

Early morning at the café . . .

Did you speak to your friend about Frank?

Yes. He's coming here at lunch time.

49

Mr. Brashov wants to talk to Frank.

Is everything all right?

Yes. My friend at the post office garage needs a mechanic. He's coming here to meet you.

50

I have an interview today? Look at me! My clothes! I need a shave. I don't even have a résumé anymore.

Don't worry. We are going to help you.

51

Everyone helps Frank get ready for the interview.

52

53

I think you are ready.

Don't worry. You look great.

54

You'll do fine.

Here's your résumé.

55

56

57

58

59

60

61

62

63

64

65

66

67

Jamal gives Jihan some flowers.

68

69

A few days later at the café . . .

70

71

72

Tell the Story

Put the pictures and sentences in order. Number 1 to 8. Then tell the story to someone.

_____ a.

Jess introduces Frank to Marty.

_____ b.

Rosa helps Frank get ready for his interview.

_____ c.

Frank fixes the lights for Mr. Brashov.

_____ d.

The café workers think the man is a robber.

_____ e.

Frank tells everyone he got the job.

_____ f.

Frank has a difficult time in his interview.

_1_ g.

A man sits on a bench.

_____ h.

Katherine tries to help Frank.

Search

Unscramble the word. Complete the sentence.

1. The man was _____laid off_____ from his job. (d l a i   f o f)

2. A person who works on cars is a _____. (i m h a c e n c)

3. The store manager wants to _____ many people for the job. (w e i t n r e v i)

4. Cars are made at a _____. (f y r a t c o)

5. Many _____ leave from the large airport every day. (l t g s i f h)

Now find each word below. When you find a word, circle it.

```
I  N  T  E  R  V  I  E  W  N
X  S  M  F  W  F  G  H  P  S
G  L  E  A  N  E  P  L  U  T
F  A  C  T  O  R  Y  M  R  Q
H  I  H  B  L  V  A  D  V  W
L  D  A  C  P  O  B  C  N  O
Y  O  N  D  I  K  P  U  J  K
R  F  I  E  P  J  I  Q  T  I
Z  F  C  F  L  I  G  H  T  S
```

Build Your Vocabulary

A Hotel Room

Read the words in the list. Find the numbers in the picture.

1. drapes
2. lamp
3. bedspread
4. window
5. couch
6. double bed
7. paintings
8. crib
9. night stand
10. pillows

Complete the sentences. Use the words from the picture.

1. The lamp is on the ____night stand (10)____.

2. In the morning, the sun shines through the _____.

3. There are two _____ hanging on the wall.

4. A bed for two people is called a _____.

5. On top of the bed there is a _____.

6. The baby sleeps in the _____.

7. People put _____ under their heads when they sleep.

8. The _____ are hanging on the window.

9. There is a _____ next to the bed.

10. The _____ is below the paintings.

Picture Dictionary

Study the picture and the English word. Copy the word. Then you may write the word in your language.

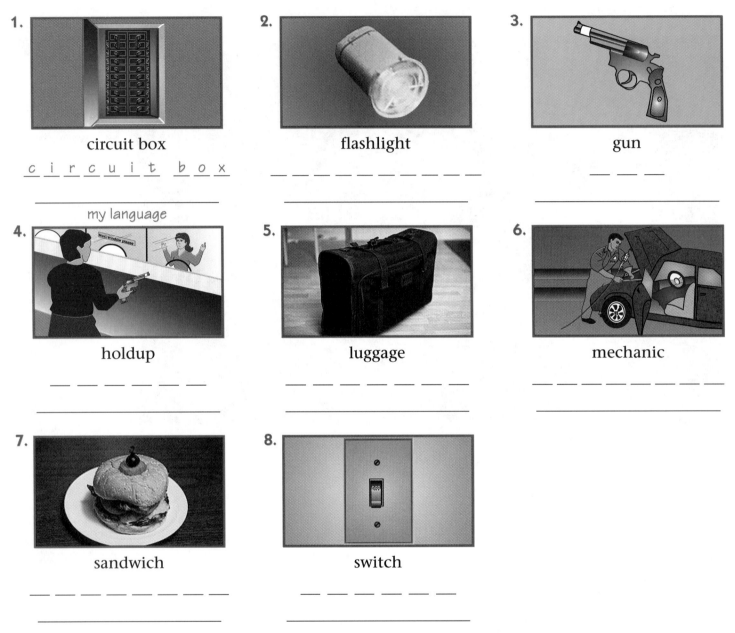

1.

circuit box

c i r c u i t   b o x

_____

my language

2.

flashlight

_ _ _ _ _ _ _ _ _

_____

3.

gun

_ _ _

_____

4.

holdup

_ _ _ _ _ _

_____

5.

luggage

_ _ _ _ _ _ _

_____

6.

mechanic

_ _ _ _ _ _ _ _

_____

7.

sandwich

_ _ _ _ _ _ _ _

_____

8.

switch

_ _ _ _ _ _

_____

Glossary

fill in: to act in someone's place. *When a music teacher is ill, another teacher fills in and teaches the class.*

flight: a trip by air. *Many flights are delayed because of heavy snow.*

give up: to stop. *Don't give up your dream of becoming a teacher.*

minimum wage: the lowest amount of money per hour that an employer can pay a worker. *Many years ago, the minimum wage was $2.75 per hour.*

post office: a place which takes care of mail and sells stamps. *Every day, the post office worker delivers mail to the apartment building.*

temporary: something that is not lasting or permanent. *The job opening at the restaurant is temporary; the regular cook will return in one month.*

23 The Gift

It is Victor Brashov's 65th birthday. There are many surprises. The workers plan a surprise for him. He surprises the workers and his daughter. His daughter surprises him.

What are the surprises?

Who's in This Story?

Victor Brashov
the café owner

Joe
Victor's friend
a café customer

Emery Bradford
an accountant

Anna Brashov
Victor's daughter

Elizabeth
Anna's daughter
Victor's granddaughter

Jamal
the handyman

Henry
the busboy

Jess
a regular customer

Katherine
the waitress

Rosa
the cook

1

Hi, everybody.

2

Henry!

The party is a surprise.

What's a birthday party without balloons?

3

How are you going to hide them?

I'm not. I have to go to school. See you later.

4

Crossroads Café . . . Hello? . . . Hello?

5

Good morning, Mr. Brashov.

This is a beautiful day.

6

7

8

9

10

✓ **Check Yourself**

1. Why are the workers at the café early?
   a. to prepare a surprise party for Mr. Brashov
   b. to prepare the restaurant for customers

2. How does Mr. Brashov feel?
   a. He is happy because everyone remembers his birthday.
   b. He is disappointed because everyone forgets his birthday.

11

12

13

14

15

16

17

18

19 Joe returns to the café.

Our cabin is open this weekend. You're welcome to use it.

That is very nice of you, Joe, but I can't. I have too much work to do here.

20

The cabin is only two hours from here.

Well, I have no plans. Maybe I will use it.

21 Katherine and Rosa worry that Mr. Brashov will miss their surprise party for him.

22

Excuse me, Mr. Brashov, but I have all the receipts for this week.

And I have all the supply and food invoices ready.

23

I will take my work with me to the lake.

Walk down to the office with me. We'll get the brochure with the directions.

24 Mr. Brashov leaves with Joe, and Jess arrives.

Is everything ready for Victor's surprise party?

Yes, but Mr. Brashov is talking about going to the lake tonight.

Don't worry. We'll keep him here.

✓ Check Yourself

3. Why does Joe return to the café?
   a. He wants to invite Mr. Brashov to his cabin.
   b. He wants to wish Mr. Brashov a happy birthday.
4. Why do Rosa and Katherine tell Mr. Brashov he has work to do?
   a. They don't want him to go to the lake.
   b. They don't want to do the work for him.

25

Later in Mr. Brashov's office . . .

Will this letter keep Mr. Brashov here?

I think so. It only needs to sound official.

26

Hurry. Mr. Brashov is coming back!

27

Mr. Brashov returns with a brochure.

I am going to take a little vacation.

28

I heard. You will have a great time.

Here's the mail, Mr. Brashov.

Bills. They can wait until Monday.

29

Oh no! Something from the Internal Revenue Service.

30

37

I'll take the cake out of the freezer. Don't worry. He won't see a thing.

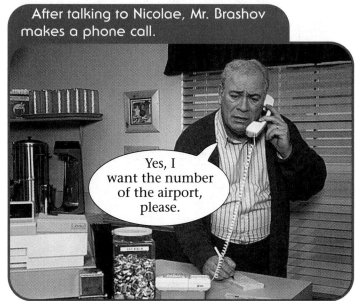

38

After talking to Nicolae, Mr. Brashov makes a phone call.

Yes, I want the number of the airport, please.

39

I found that receipt.

Wonderful. I'll be right back.

40

Mr. Bradford leaves for a few minutes.

41

42

✔ **Check Yourself**

5. Why does Jess use the typewriter?
   a. to write a letter to his son
   b. to write a letter to Mr. Brashov

6. Why do the workers want Emery Bradford to come?
   a. so Mr. Brashov can go to the lake Friday night
   b. so Mr. Brashov will not go to the lake Friday night

Later that night at Crossroads Café . . .

43

Surprise!

44

Where's Victor?

I don't know. He left a note.

45

It says, "Forgive me for leaving. I had to take care of some important business."

46

Wait. He took a call on the phone by the cash register.

Let's go look.

47

They find a phone number and Jess dials it.

48

49

50

51

52

53

54

55 Mr. Brashov's friends arrive at the airport.

Look!

56 Hello, Anna.

Mr. Washington.

57 What is going on here?

Baggage Claim

It is a long story.

58 Tell us about it at the café.

Why at the café?

Because an airport is no place to celebrate a birthday.

59 I thought you all forgot.

That's a long story, too.

60 Anna, why don't you come with us?

No, I have to work.

61

62

63

64

65

66

67

I have a wonderful idea. Stay at my house tonight. Tomorrow, we can go to a lake in the mountains.

68

No, you don't, Mr. Brashov.

Wait. I forgot. I have to meet with the IRS on Monday.

69

That was all part of the joke.

Joke?

70

Happy birthday, Mr. Brashov.

71

✓ **Check Yourself**

9. What gift does Anna bring to her father?
   a. her daughter
   b. a watch

10. Can Mr. Brashov go to the lake?
    a. No. He meets with the IRS on Monday.
    b. Yes. The letter wasn't really from the IRS.

72

Tell the Story

Match the picture with the sentence. Then tell the story to someone.

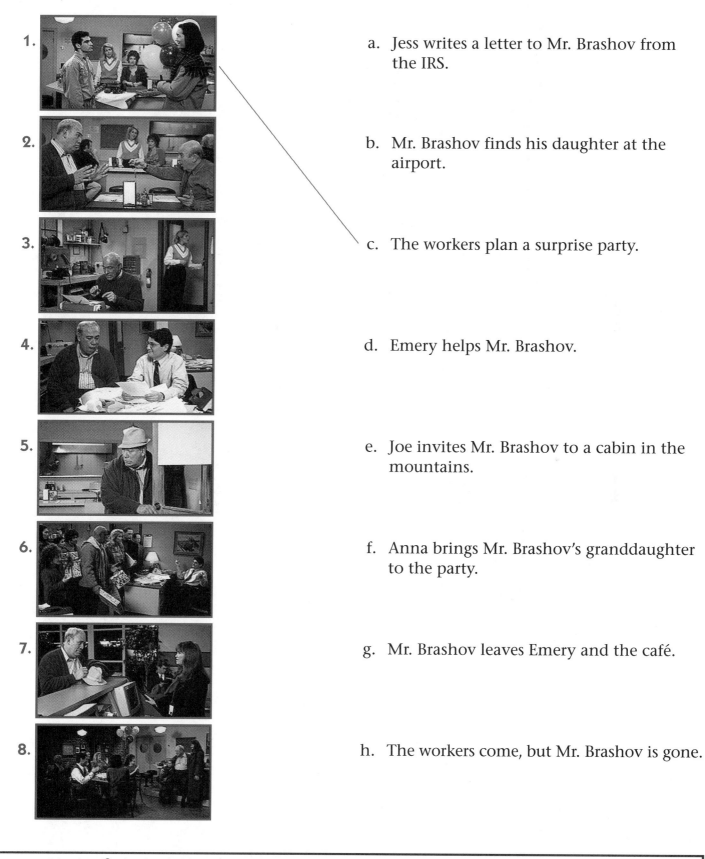

1.

2.

3.

4.

5.

6.

7.

8.

a. Jess writes a letter to Mr. Brashov from the IRS.

b. Mr. Brashov finds his daughter at the airport.

c. The workers plan a surprise party.

d. Emery helps Mr. Brashov.

e. Joe invites Mr. Brashov to a cabin in the mountains.

f. Anna brings Mr. Brashov's granddaughter to the party.

g. Mr. Brashov leaves Emery and the café.

h. The workers come, but Mr. Brashov is gone.

Search

For each sentence in the box, write the number in a circle.

> 1. His friends forget his birthday.
>
> 2. His friends say *no* to his dinner invitation.
>
> 3. His brother calls to wish him a happy birthday.
>
> 4. He misses his family.
>
> 5. He gets a letter from the IRS.
>
> 6. He visits his daughter.
>
> 7. His friends give him a party.
>
> 8. He sees his granddaughter.

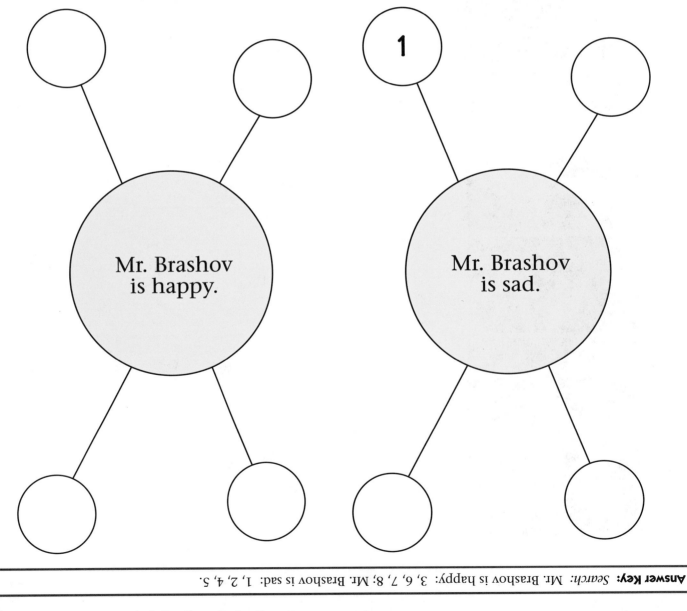

Build Your Vocabulary

An Airport

Read the words in the list. Find the numbers in the picture.

1. ticket agents
2. ticket counter
3. gate
4. airplane
5. suitcase
6. ticket
7. passengers

Complete the sentences. Use the words from the picture.

1. There are three passengers standing in line at the ___ticket counter (2)___.

2. One of the passengers at the ticket counter has her coat over her arm and her _____ in her hand.

3. From the window, the passengers can see the _____.

4. The lady sitting behind the passengers in line has a _____.

5. Seven _____ sitting in the waiting area are waiting to get on their plane.

6. The two airline employees behind the counter work as _____.

7. The airline employee standing near the _____ will take passengers' tickets when they get on the plane.

Picture Dictionary

Study the picture and the English word. Copy the word. Then you may write the word in your language.

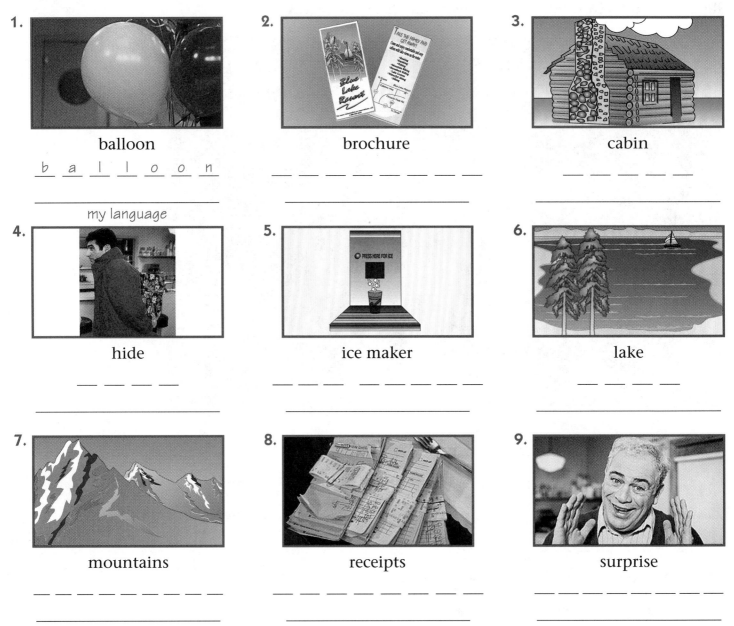

1. balloon

b a l l o o n

_____

my language

2. brochure

_____

3. cabin

_____

4. hide

_____

5. ice maker

_____

6. lake

_____

7. mountains

_____

8. receipts

_____

9. surprise

_____

Glossary

celebrate: to have a good time with others for a special reason. *We celebrate birthdays with cakes and candles.*

forget: unable to remember. *His wife gets angry when he forgets her birthday.*

Internal Revenue Service (IRS): the government agency that collects taxes. *You need to send your tax forms to the IRS by April 15.*

joke: trick for fun. *When he telephoned, he said he was somebody else. I didn't think his joke was funny.*

remember: recall, think of again. *Did you remember to mail the letters I gave you?*

taxes: money people have to pay to the government. *Before you get your paycheck, the boss will take out money for income tax.*

24 All's Well That Ends Well

Katherine and Bill are getting married tomorrow. Tonight there is a party at the café. Katherine is upset because there are some problems.

What are the problems?

Who's in This Story?

Katherine
the café waitress

Bill Macelli
Katherine's fiancé

David
Katherine's teenage son

Suzanne
Katherine's daughter

Henry
the busboy and
delivery person

Calli
a taxi cab driver

Lars Sorenson
Katherine's grandfather

Uncle Antonio
Bill's uncle

Aunt Sophia
Bill's aunt

Aunt Josephine
Bill's aunt

Rosa
the cook

Victor Brashov
the café owner

Jamal
the handyman

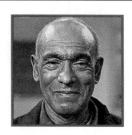

Jess
a regular customer

1

2

3

4

5

6

Katherine's two children, David and Suzanne, are cooking in the kitchen.

Let me do it!

No, you did the last one!

7

Rosa, what are you going to do with the box?

I'll put it in the back room.

8

Oh, no!!

9

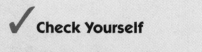

✓ **Check Yourself**

1. What are the workers doing?
   a. cleaning the café
   b. getting ready for a party

2. What does the delivery man bring to the café?
   a. a wedding dress
   b. flowers

10

Oh, boy!

Oh, big boy!

Katherine needs to start eating right away.

11

Mr. Brashov answers the phone.

Crossroads Café . . . No, Katherine Blake is not here. I'll give her a message. What? But the wedding is tomorrow afternoon!

12

13

14

15

16

17

18

19

20

21

22

23

24

31 Katherine's friends hear her scream.

✓ **Check Yourself**

5. Why is Suzanne unhappy?
   a. because she wants to talk to her mother
   b. because she lost the wedding ring

6. What is the problem with Katherine's wedding dress?
   a. It is too big.
   b. It is the wrong color.

32

33 Katherine runs to the bathroom and locks the door.

Come on, honey. Everything will be O.K. Please come out.

NO!!!

Please?

34

Katherine, it's just me out here. You can come out. The dress can't be that bad.

35 Katherine talks to Rosa from the bathroom.

Yes, it is awful.

Trust me, Katherine. Please come out.

36 A few minutes later . . .

Well, Rosa, what do you think?

I think we need a lot of help.

Everyone listens to the radio.

. . . This city is slowing down because of the snow. In some areas, there is no electricity. The airport may close in . . .

37

When? When will the airport close?

38

Mr. Brashov takes some money from the cash register.

What are you doing, Mr. Brashov?

I am getting some money for Henry.

39

Henry, you are going to the airport to pick up Katherine's grandfather. The money is for the taxi.

40

Henry leaves the café and gets into a taxicab.

Please, take me to the airport.

No problem. We'll be there quickly.

41

I need to go to the International Terminal.

No problem.

42

43

A little while later at the café . . .

Bill, your father called. He says that he will be a little late.

O.K. Thanks.

. . . and, there are a lot of cars arriving at the café.

44

Katherine is still in the bathroom.

Katherine, my family is here. They really want to meet you. Can you please come out now?

No!

45

Mr. Brashov welcomes guests to the café.

Welcome, welcome! Come in. It's nice to meet you.

It's a pleasure. I am Antonio, Bill's uncle. Where's the bride?

46

Uncle Antonio thinks that Rosa is Katherine.

Katherine, give me a big hug. Welcome to the family.

47

A little while later in the taxi . . .

Calli, wait! There is a sign for the airport! Pull over please.

48

Henry and Calli pick up a man at the airport, but he is the wrong man.

Later that evening at the café . . .

49

Aunt Josephine! It's great to see you! Did you have any trouble getting here?

What do **you** think?

50

So, where is the bride?

Yes, where is Katherine? I want to meet her.

Well, Katherine wants to meet all of you. She is, uh . . . well, she is . . .

51

She's not here because . . . she went home to get her wedding dress.

52

✓ Check Yourself

7. Why does Henry leave the café?

   a. to pick up flowers for the wedding

   b. to meet Katherine's grandfather at the airport

8. Why does Bill want Katherine to come out of the bathroom?

   a. to meet his family

   b. to dance with him

53

A little while later, Henry finally meets Katherine's grandfather, Lars Sorenson.

Is there a problem with the taxi? It's bouncing. Why don't you pull over to the side of the road?

O.K.

54

Jamal leaves Katherine and returns to the guests.

Excuse me, ladies and gentlemen. I just spoke to Katherine. She will be here soon.

61

Hi, everybody!

62

What happened?

It's a long story. We . . .

Never mind. I can only imagine.

63

This is Calli, our taxi driver.

It's a pleasure to be here.

64

And this is Katherine's grandfather, Lars Sorenson.

Papa Lars!

Hi! Where's my Katrina?

65

Hi, Grandpa!

66

67

Katrina?

Grandpa!

68

A little while later . . .

A toast to the bride and groom . . . Tomorrow is their wedding day. May they have a long and happy life together.

69

Aunt Sophia eats some pastry.

Who made this pastry? It's as hard as a rock!

70

There's the wedding ring! I told you I didn't lose it.

71

 Check Yourself

9. Why is Katherine late to the party?

   a. She came from the airport.

   b. She locked herself in the bathroom.

10. Where does Aunt Sophia find the wedding ring?

   a. under the table

   b. in the pastry

72

Tell the Story

Put the pictures and sentences in order. Number 1 to 8. Then tell the story to someone.

___ a.

Katherine is sad about her dress.

___ b.

Mr. Brashov makes a toast
to Bill and Katherine.

___ c.

Henry goes to the airport to meet
Katherine's grandfather.

___ d.

Katherine is glad to see her grandfather.

___ e.

Mr. Brashov welcomes people
to the café.

1 f.

Katherine's friends at Crossroads Café
get ready for a party.

___ g.

Aunt Sophia finds the wedding ring.

___ h.

The delivery man brings Katherine's
dress to the café.

Search

For each sentence in the box, write the number in a circle.

1. The photographer is sick.

2. Mr. Brashov makes a toast to Katherine and Bill.

3. Katherine sees her grandfather.

4. The airport may close.

5. Aunt Sophia finds the wedding ring.

6. Katherine's wedding dress is too big.

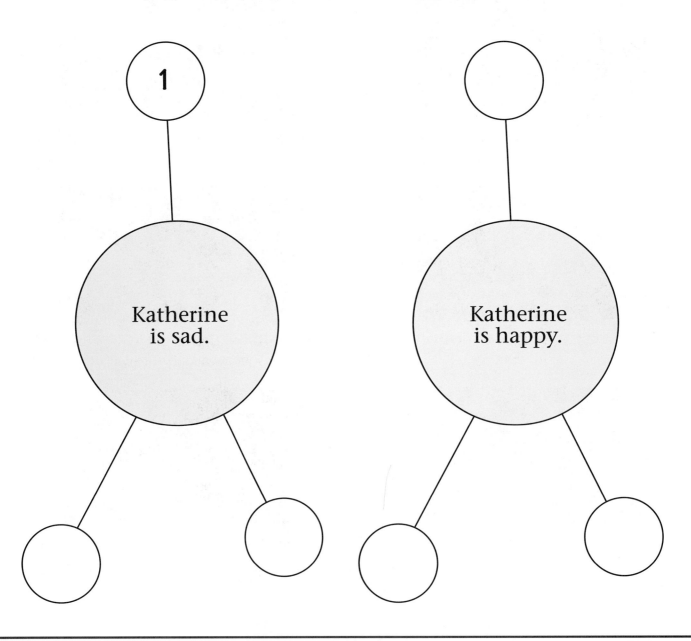

Build Your Vocabulary

In the Kitchen

Read the words in the list. Find the numbers in the picture.

1. apron
2. mixing bowl
3. eggs
4. electric mixer
5. batter
6. spoon
7. sugar
8. beaters
9. rolling pin

Complete the sentences. Use the words from the picture.

1. There is a box of _____sugar (7)_____ near the little cakes.

2. Suzanne put all the ingredients in a large _____.

3. A wooden tool with two handles used to roll dough flat is a _____.

4. David is wearing an _____ over his clothes.

5. Suzanne has a _____ in her hand to mix things in the bowl.

6. An easier way to mix things is to use an _____.

7. You can take the _____ out of the electric mixer to wash them.

8. There is a carton with 12 _____ on the counter.

9. Suzanne is preparing the cake _____, which is made of sugar, flour, butter, and eggs.

Picture Dictionary

Study the picture and the English word. Copy the word. Then you may write the word in your language.

1. airport

a i r p o r t

_____
my language

2. box

_ _ _

_____

3. bride

_ _ _ _ _

_____

4. groom

_ _ _ _ _

_____

5. photographer

_ _ _ _ _ _ _ _ _ _ _ _

_____

6. ring bearer

_ _ _ _   _ _ _ _ _ _

_____

7. taxicab

_ _ _ _ _ _ _

_____

8. tire

_ _ _ _

_____

9. wedding ring

_ _ _ _ _ _ _   _ _ _ _

_____

Glossary

awful: bad, terrible. *The awful snowstorm caused the roads to be very slippery.*

fix: repair. *She asked the mechanic to fix her car quickly because she needs to use it tomorrow.*

nervous: worried or uncomfortable about something. *The singer always feels nervous before she sings in front of a crowd.*

pastry: a mixture of flour, butter, and other things used to make pies or other foods. *She needs two large pieces of pastry and eight apples for her apple pie.*

surprise: A feeling of wonder or shock when something happens that is unexpected. *When the young man finishes college, his parents have a nice surprise for him: a new car.*

terminal: buildings where people wait for buses, trains, or airplanes. *The travelers had to wait in the airport terminal because there was a problem with their plane.*

25 Comings and Goings

There are changes at Crossroads Café.
The workers feel both happy and sad.

Why do they feel this way?

Who's in This Story?

Katherine
the café waitress

Danny Finkelman
a record producer

Abdullah
a friend of Jamal

Jihan
Jamal's wife

Rob
a band member
Henry's friend

Marie Angeloux
a job applicant

Henry
the busboy and
delivery person

Victor Brashov
the café owner

Rosa
the cook

Jess
a regular customer

Jamal
the handyman

1

2

3

4

5

6

The record producer listens to the tape of Henry's band.

Not bad, not bad at all.

7

I hear bands all day. A lot of them sound good. Just like you.

8

Almost anyone can sound good on a tape. But how will you sound in front of 20,000 people?

9

Where do you play?

We play live concerts. Come listen to us.

We play at Crossroads Café all the time.

10

Henry works there after school.

When I sign a record contract, I am finished with school.

11

✓ **Check Yourself**

1. Who is leaving the café?
   a. Henry
   b. Katherine

2. Why does Henry go to Danny's office?
   a. He wants a record contract.
   b. He delivers food to Danny.

12

13

14

15

Katherine is interviewing people for the waitress job.

16

17

18

19

20

21

22

23

24

25

26

27

28

It's too bad you're not in Egypt, Jamal.

Why?

I would like to offer you the job as chief engineer.

29

30

31

The next morning at Jamal and Jihan's apartment . . .

I couldn't sleep last night.

I couldn't either.

32

Every day I feel less like a man. Will I have to tell our child that I am a handyman?

I know, but . . .

Jihan, you're not listening. I can not do this anymore.

33

Later that morning, Katherine interviews another woman for the waitress job.

34

That was terrific!

Thank you.

35

Where did you work before?

Oh, at many restaurants.

Thanks for coming in. I'll let you know.

36

So, how was she?

Great. But I'm still looking.

37

38

39

40

41

42

Later at the café . . .

I'd like you to meet Crossroads Café's new waitress: Marie.

It's nice to meet you.

49

Henry walks into the café.

Marie, this is Henry Chang: busboy, delivery boy, and future rock star.

50

Henry. I heard you were great. Sorry I couldn't come.

That's O.K., Mr. Washington.

51

Finally. I thought you forgot about our game.

I'm sorry, Jess. There's so much paperwork to do.

52

Victor, you have to slow down. Leave time for the important things.

Like our chess game?

Exactly.

53

Katherine, I can't believe you're really leaving.

I hope you and Carol are coming to the going away party tonight.

We wouldn't miss it for anything.

54

Jamal talks on the phone in the back room.

Abdullah, We cannot decide. All right . . . I will call you soon.

55

Mr. Brashov and Jess continue with their game.

56

A delivery man enters the café.

57

I'm sorry, Jess. I need to talk to the delivery man.

I'm going home.

What about our game?

58

We can play another time.

After the party tonight, we can finish.

59

✓ **Check Yourself**

7. Who is the new waitress?
   a. Marie
   b. Katherine

8. What does Jess want Mr. Brashov to do?
   a. to have coffee with him
   b. to finish the chess game

60

61 Later that night at Katherine's party . . .

62 This is a wonderful party, Mr. Brashov. I wish Jess and Carol were here.

They will be here soon.

63 Jamal and Jihan talk about Egypt.

I want **us** to make the decision.

Whatever decision we make, one of us will be unhappy.

64 I want to thank Katherine for all her hard work at Crossroads Café. I wish her the best of luck.

65

66 Mr. Brashov answers the phone.

Hello . . . ah, Carol. Finally. Where are you?

What did you say?

67

That was Carol. Jess was in a car accident. He was driving home when a car hit him.

68

Jess died about an hour ago.

69

70

71

✓ **Check Yourself**

9. Who makes a speech about Katherine?
   a. Mr. Brashov
   b. Rosa

10. Why didn't Carol and Jess come to the party?
    a. They have a problem with their car.
    b. Jess died in a car accident.

72

Tell the Story

Put the pictures and sentences in order. For each story, number 1 to 3. Then tell each story to someone.

Katherine's Story

_____ a.

Katherine introduces the new waitress.

_____ b.

Mr. Brashov wishes Katherine good luck.

__1__ c.

Katherine interviews people for the waitress job.

Henry's Story

_____ a.

Henry's band plays at Crossroads Café.

_____ b.

Danny listens to Henry's tape.

_____ c.

Danny tells Henry that he won't give him a record contract.

Search

For each sentence in the box, write the number in a circle.

1. Katherine is leaving the café.

2. Mr. Brashov plays chess with Jess.

3. Jess dies in a car accident.

4. Mr. Brashov can't play chess because he's too busy.

5. There are no problems at Henry's concert.

6. Mr. Brashov wishes Katherine good luck at her party.

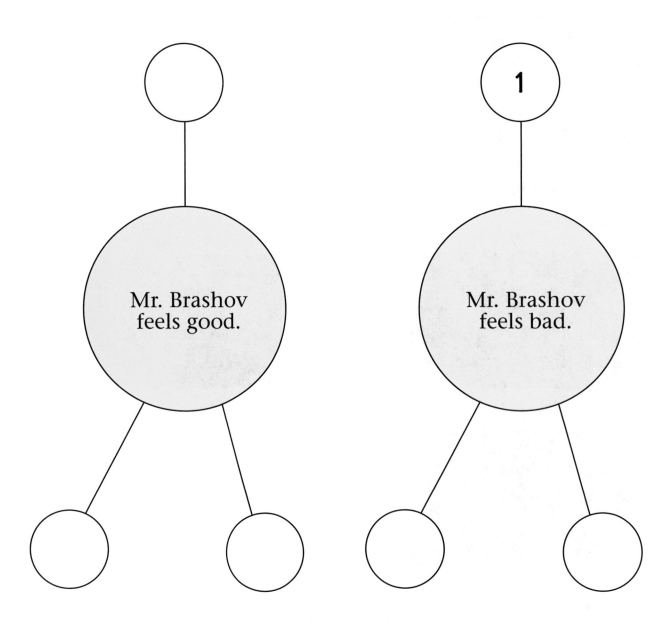

Build Your Vocabulary

A Concert

Read the words in the list. Find the numbers in the picture.

1. guitar
2. lights
3. stage
4. microphone
5. drums
6. speakers
7. musicians

Complete the sentences. Use the words from the picture.

1. Henry has the _____microphone (4)_____ in his hand.

2. The band has large _____ so that everyone in the room can hear the music.

3. Rob is holding an electric _____.

4. The musician is standing behind a set of _____.

5. The band members put their equipment on a wooden _____.

6. There are four _____ in the band.

7. There are five _____ shining over the stage.

Picture Dictionary

Study the picture and the English word. Copy the word. Then you may write the word in your language.

1.

auto accident

<u>a u t o   a c c i d e n t</u>

_____
my language

2.

band

_ _ _ _

_____

3.

office

_ _ _ _ _ _

_____

4.

party

_ _ _ _ _

_____

5.

tape

_ _ _ _

_____

Glossary

concert: a musical event. *The singer and his band performed concerts to raise money for the poor.*

confident: a feeling that a person can do something well. *The boss at the factory sees that his new worker is very confident on the job.*

contract: an agreement written and signed by those who make it. *People sign contracts when they buy and sell cars or houses.*

drop out: to leave or stop taking part in. *He wants to drop out of school so he can get a job.*

famous: very well known. *She is a famous author who has written many children's books.*

replacement: a person who takes the job of another. *If a soccer player gets hurt during a game, a replacement plays for her.*

26 Winds of Change

The Crossroads Café workers make plans
for the future. They make decisions about
schools, jobs, and their personal lives.

What does each one decide to do?

Who's in This Story?

Carol Washington
Jess's wife

Derek Washington
Carol and Jess's son

Mr. Clayborne
a business man

Victor Brashov
the café owner

Jess
a regular customer

Rosa
the cook

Jamal
the handyman

Henry
the busboy and
delivery person

Jihan
Jamal's wife

Marie
the new waitress

Katherine
the former waitress

1

2

5

6

The next day at the Washington house . . .

This card is from Sally.

She's the lady down the street.

14

There is a knock at the door.

Victor, please come in.

I hope I am not disturbing you.

No, not at all.

15

Derek, this is Mr. Brashov. He's the owner of the café where your father spent so much time.

16

He talked about you a lot.

Your father was a wonderful man.

17

Mr. Brashov and Carol sit down and talk.

Jess and I spent so much time playing chess. I want to give you this.

18

19

Why don't you keep it?

No, it should be here.

20

Carol puts the chess set on the coffee table.

I don't know if I feel better or worse when I look at his things.

21

Carol, if you need anything . . .

The only thing I need is more time with Jess. And you can't give me that.

22

For years, we talked about going on a cruise. He wanted to show me the Greek islands. But we never went.

23

I finally bought the tickets. I was going to surprise Jess on our next anniversary.

I'm sorry, Carol. Maybe you and your son should go.

It's not the same.

24

I have to get back to the café. Good-bye.

25

✓ **Check Yourself**

3. Who does Mr. Brashov meet at Carol's home?
   a. Jamal
   b. Derek

4. What does Mr. Brashov give Carol?
   a. a card
   b. a chess set

26

A few days later at the café . . .

Jamal, what's in the box?

My tools. I'm sending them to Egypt. We changed our minds again.

27

Katherine comes into the café.

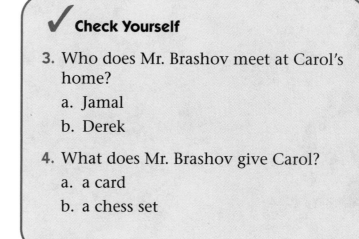

Hey, look who's here!

Hi, Henry.

28

So, how's life?

Absolutely terrific!

29

What's this?

It's the catalogue from City College. I have to take a few more classes before I start law school.

30

A little while later, Henry cuts his hand.

31

Where are the first aid supplies?

In Mr. Brashov's office.

32

Come on, Henry. Rosa, are you O.K. out here?

I think so.

I'll take care of the customers.

33

Marie helps Henry.

You should be more careful.

But you always tell me to work faster.

Faster is not another word for careless.

34

Marie finishes with Henry's hand.

Do I need stitches?

No. But keep it clean. I'll look at it again tomorrow.

35

You did a nice job. Just like a nurse . . .

I am a nurse.

36

37 But I need a certificate to work in this country. So, I have to study more.

38 **You** don't have to worry about that. With your job at Crossroads Café, nobody will care about your education.

39 I'm not going to be here forever.

Where are you going to go? There aren't many opportunities for a bus boy with a high school education.

Marie returns to the dining room.

40 Thanks for helping out.

Any time.

Carol Washington comes into the café.

41 Hello, Carol. Come in.

Sure. We can go into my office.

Victor, I'd like to talk to you. Do you have a minute?

Henry picks up Katherine's college catalogue.

42

Carol and Mr. Brashov talk in the utility room.

Victor, there's something I want you to have.

43

Carol hands some tickets to Mr. Brashov.

I can't take these.

Why not?

Because they are your tickets. Taking a trip would be the best thing in the world for you.

44

I can't. I would think about Jess all the time. This would make Jess very happy.

45

When would I go?

Don't wait for the perfect time. It may never come . . . Please take them. For Jess.

All right. For Jess.

46

Later, Mr. Brashov has a meeting with a businessman.

So, they usually make deliveries twice a week?

Unless we are very busy. Then they will make an extra delivery.

47

All right. I think I have everything I need.

Please call me if you have any questions.

48

49

Mr. Brashov wants to talk to everybody.

I made an important decision. I am going to sell Crossroads Café. . . . The man who just left will be the new owner. His name is Mr. Clayborne.

50

I don't understand.

Henry, I am 65 years old. I want to spend time with my daughter and granddaughter. I want to visit my brother. So, I must say good-bye to Crossroads Café.

51

So . . . when is Mr. Clayborne going to buy the café?

In a few weeks. Don't worry about him. He's very fair and honest.

52

One week later . . .

My lawyer will have everything ready in a day or two.

Tell him to take his time. I want everything to go well.

53

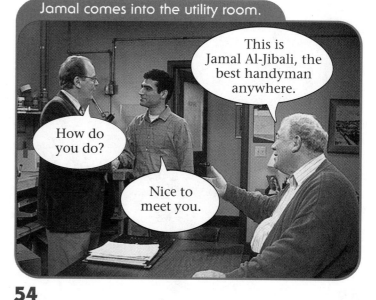

Jamal comes into the utility room.

This is Jamal Al-Jibali, the best handyman anywhere.

How do you do?

Nice to meet you.

54

55

56

57

58

59

60

61

62

Mr. Brashov and Mr. Clayborne finish their meeting.

Thank you for coming in.

I hope you won't be sorry, Mr. Brashov.

It's the right decision. Good luck, Mr. Clayborne.

63

So, when does the new boss start?

Rosa, Mr. Clayborne is not going to buy Crossroads Café.

What? Did he change his mind?

No, I did.

64

But, what about all the things you want to do?

I am still going to do them.

65

How? I'm confused.

I know someone who can manage the restaurant for me.

How did you find this person so fast?

66

This person is very smart, very ambitious, has experience in the restaurant business, and is someone I trust completely.

This person is perfect.

67

Mr. Brashov gives some keys to Rosa.

What are these for?

If you are going to manage Crossroads Café, you have to open the door.

You're not serious.

68

I am very serious and very happy for both of us. See you tomorrow.

But what about the supply order?

You know what to do.

69

What about hiring someone to replace Jamal? . . . I have so many questions.

Don't worry, Rosa. We'll talk about everything in the morning. And we can talk more when I return.

70

Return? From where?

My daughter, granddaughter, and I are taking a trip to the Greek Islands.

71

Mr. Brashov leaves the café. Rosa thinks about her new job.

Yes!!!

72

✓ **Check Yourself**

9. Who is the new manager of the café?
   a. Mr. Clayborne
   b. Rosa

10. How does Rosa feel now?
   a. happy
   b. angry

Tell the Story

Put the pictures and sentences in order. For each story, number 1 to 3. Then tell each story to someone.

Henry's Story

____ a.

Henry looks at a college catalogue.

____ b.

Marie is happy because Henry is going to college.

__1__ c.

Marie is unhappy with Henry because he is late.

Mr. Brashov's Story

____ a.

Mr. Brashov asks Rosa to be the new manager of the café.

____ b.

Mr. Clayborne talks to Mr. Brashov about buying the café.

____ c.

Mr. Brashov tells Rosa that he won't sell the café.

Search

Read each group of words that describe a person's future plans. Put a check (✓) under the correct person.

	Mr. Brashov	Rosa	Henry	Katherine	Jamal
1. Will hire a new handyman		✓			
2. Will go to college for the first time					
3. Will go on a cruise					
4. Will begin a new engineering job					
5. Will go to law school					
6. Will spend time with daughter and granddaughter					
7. Will be the new café manager					
8. Will move to Egypt					
9. Will spend time with Bill and the kids					

Build Your Vocabulary

First Aid Supplies

Read the words in the list. Find the numbers in the picture.

1. bandage
2. Band Aids®
3. surgical tape
4. first aid kit
5. scissors
6. gloves
7. towel

Complete the sentences. Use the words from the picture.

1. Marie is putting ____surgical tape (3)____ on Henry's bandage so it will stay on his hand.

2. She always wears _____ when she gives first aid.

3. Henry will have to change his _____ in a couple of days.

4. Marie uses a pair of _____ to cut the tape.

5. Mr. Brashov keeps a _____ in his office in case someone gets hurt.

6. Henry tried to stop the bleeding with a _____.

7. Marie can't use the box of _____, because Henry's cut is too big.

Picture Dictionary

Study the picture and the English word. Copy the word. Then you may write the word in your language.

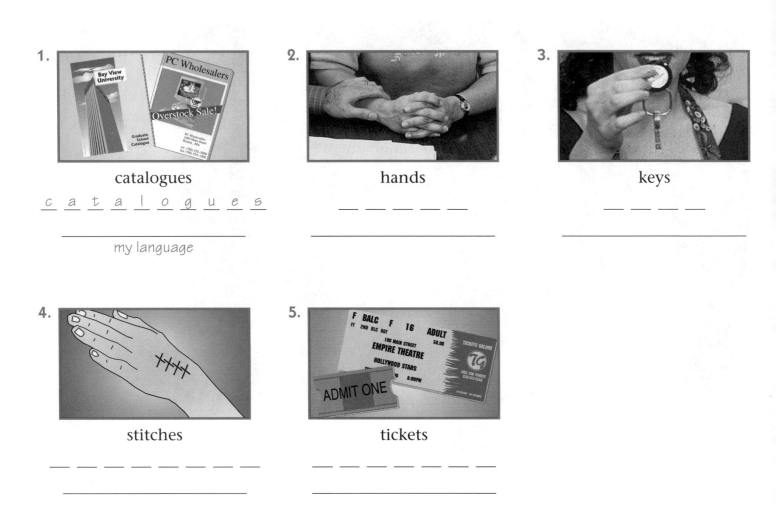

1. catalogues

c a t a l o g u e s

_____
my language

2. hands

_ _ _ _ _

_____

3. keys

_ _ _ _

_____

4. stitches

_ _ _ _ _ _ _ _

_____

5. tickets

_ _ _ _ _ _ _

_____

Glossary

ambitious: wanting success. *She is very ambitious. She wants to become a millionaire before she is thirty-five.*

careless: doing things without thinking, sometimes dangerous. *The careless young man likes to ride his motorcycle without wearing a helmet.*

cruise: a fun trip on a large boat or ship. *Many people like to go on a cruise for vacation.*

disturb: to interrupt. *Loud music always disturbs the man when he is trying to sleep.*

loyal: reliable, dependable and faithful to someone or something. *She is a loyal friend. She always helps me when I'm in trouble.*

unfair: not fair, not right. *The young man didn't do anything wrong. It was unfair that the police took him to jail.*

Teacher/Tutor Appendix

If you have read the section *To the Learner* at the beginning of this book, the information in this appendix will provide a more detailed understanding of the scope and the goals of the program. The *Crossroads Café* print and video materials are closely correlated to provide everything needed for successful, non-stressful language-learning experiences, either alone or with a teacher or tutor.

The *Worktexts*

The two *Crossroads Café Worktexts* provide multi-level language activities with three levels of challenge: Beginning High, Intermediate Low, and Intermediate High as defined by the ESL Model Standards for Adult Education Programs (Sacramento: California Department of Education, 1992); or SPL 4, 5, and 6 as defined in the competency-based, Mainstream English Language Training (MELT) Resource Package (Washington, DC: Office of Refugee Resettlement, 1985). These activities are visually designated in the *Worktext* as ★, ★★, or ★★★, respectively. The 1-star exercises ask learners to communicate using words and phrases; responses are frequently based on a visual stimulus. The 2-star exercises ask learners to communicate using learned phrases and structures; responses may be based on visual stimulus or text. The 3-star exercises are designed for students who can participate in basic conversation; responses are most often based on text, not visuals. *Worktext* unit exercises develop *story comprehension, language skills,* and *higher order thinking* and they provide practice in reading, writing, and speaking. Every *Worktext* unit opens with a photo depicting the theme of the storyline, a list of learning objectives, and a learning strategy.

Crossroads Café Worktext Framework

	Exercise Section	Purpose	★	★★	★★★
Story Comprehension (Video)	*Before You Watch*	Preview story-line vocabulary and events.	Match words with video photos to highlight key plot points.	Match sentences with photos.	Write a question about each photo.
	Focus for Watching	Provide story focus.	Answer questions about elements of main plot.	Answer additional questions about main plot.	Answer additional questions focused on details of story.
	After You Watch	Check story comprehension.	Answer yes/no questions about the story plot using same content as previous two exercises.	Arrange 3–6 sentences about story in proper sequence.	Add, in the appropriate place, 3–4 new sentences providing additional detail.
Language Development	*Your New Language*	Focus on language function and grammatical structure of the "Word Play" video segment, e.g., making promises: *I promise to. . ., I promise that I will. . . .*	Copy words or phrases into sentences conveying language functions.	Match 2 parts of 2-line exchanges, e.g., question-answer, statement-response.	Complete a fill-in-the-blank dialogue with correct grammatical structures.

	Exercise Section	Purpose	★	★★	★★★
	Discourse Exercise	Enable learners to see language flow.	Sequence a dialogue of 3–4 sentences.	Sequence a dialogue of 4–6 sentences.	Sequence a dialogue of 6–8 sentences.
	In Your Community	Develop reading skills using reading materials from the community, e.g., a lease.	Answer factual questions taken directly from reading.	Answer factual questions requiring synthesis.	Answer questions requiring inference.
	Read and Write	Develop reading skills	Identify main idea.	Identify factual details.	Identify tone or feeling.
		Determine meaning from context.	Identify words/phrases with same meaning.	Identify words/phrases that are clues to meaning.	Infer word meaning from text clues.
		Develop writing skills.	Provide basic factual information.	Provide additional detail.	Draw conclusions, express opinions, and do other analysis, synthesis, and evaluation tasks.
Thinking Skills	*What Do You Think?*	Express and support opinions.	Indicate opinions by matching or selecting from multiple-choice items.	React to characters' opinions.	Write sentences expressing and supporting your opinions.
	Culture Clips	Recall key information presented in the *Culture Clips* video segment.	Match art with sentences from the culture clip video segment.	Complete fill-in-the-blank passage on culture clip concepts.	Respond to a situation or express an opinion related to culture clip theme.
	Check Your English	Demonstrate new material mastery.	Match written words with art depicting vocabulary.	Copy words to form a sentence/question using grammatical structure(s) presented in *Your New Language.*	Complete fill-in-the-blank passage that provides a story summary.

The *Photo Stories*

The *Photo Stories* have two primary purposes:

- They serve as a preview activity for viewers with beginning-low (but not literacy-level) English proficiency by assisting them in following the main story line when they view the video. The high-success, low-stress follow-up activities in the Photo Stories are ideal motivators for this group of learners, most of whom could not access the story without this special help.

- They can be used with learners at higher levels to preview and review the story line.

The diagram below and the descriptions that follow illustrate the carefully designed, yet simple and predictable structure of the *Photo Story* episodes.

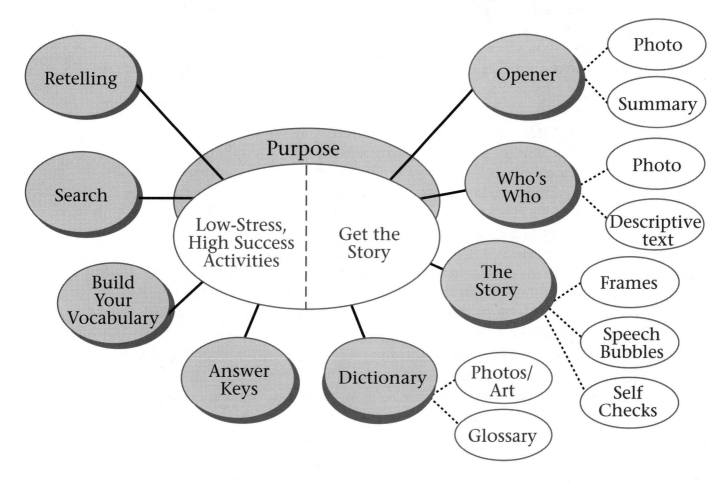

As the diagram suggests, the *Photo Stories* have a limited number of basic components, or elements:

1. **The Unit Opener:** This component helps the learner focus, using a large photo (the same one that appears at the beginning of each *Worktext* unit) that captures the theme of the episode and a capsulized summary statement of only 3 to 5 sentences that provides an overview without giving away the outcome.

2. **Who's Who:** Photos of the characters in the episode that are key to the main story line are included here. Below each photo is the character's name and a phrase describing something about the person that relates to this particular episode. For example, for Katherine in the episode "Family Matters," the phrase reads, "A single mother of two."

3. **The Story:** The story is told with photos from the episode and text, using frames and speech bubbles. Included at appropriate intervals throughout the sequence of frames are comprehension questions with which the student can self-check his or her success at "making meaning." The language "spoken" by the characters in the frames is that heard in the videos, but it is frequently simplified by deleting information, structures, and words.

4. **The Dictionary:** The dictionary provides learners with a resource for clarifying words they do not understand. It has two parts—visuals and glossary. The visuals—photos or art—may be objects, emotions, or actions that can be visually portrayed. The glossary contains six or fewer words that learners encounter in the frames. These words are not easily depicted visually and may require some explanation. The definitions given are very brief and simple. In addition, for each word in the glossary, a sentence other than the one in the video story is provided to model usage.

5. **The Activity Pages:** There are three types of activity pages—Retelling, Searches, and Build Your Vocabulary. In the Retelling activities, learners sequence pictures that represent key elements in the story. The Searches check comprehension of more detailed information, but still focus on the main theme or story line. Answers may be based on text and photo, photo only, or text only. In Build Your Vocabulary, the exercises center around a large picture that shows a scene from the story. The scene selected is rich in vocabulary that is useful to learners but not crucial to the main plot. Items in the picture are numbered, and a vocabulary list keyed to the numbers is provided. Below the pictures and vocabulary list, a series of sentences with blanks in them provides opportunities for learners to put each word into context.

6. **The Answer Keys:** The answers to all activity pages are printed upside down at the bottom of the page on which the exercise falls. The exception is the Check Yourself comprehension questions, whose answers are grouped together on the bottom of the first activity page.

In this way, through a well-designed combination of pictures, text, and language-learning activities, the *Photo Stories* teach basic language and reading-comprehension skills—thus propelling beginning low ESL learners toward higher levels of understanding and fluency.

Teacher's Resource Books

To help classroom teachers and distance-learning instructors give students all the help they need, each of the two *Crossroads Café Teacher's Resource Books* provides general directions for how to work with the program and specific instructions for how to use each episode. Each also has 52 reproducible master activities—4 for each of the 13 episodes in the book—for teachers to copy and give to students to complete in pairs and small groups. By working through these activities, students will be able to engage one another interactively. The following pages are examples of the type of guidance for teachers and activities for students that the *Teacher's Resource Books* provide. With these tools, teachers can make the most effective use of the *Crossroads Café* program during class time.

CLASS OPENER

Refer to suggestions on page xx of the Introduction.

YOUR NEW LANGUAGE

Replay **Word Play** (18:14–19:52) **before** learners complete this section of the worktext. To introduce the language focus use a map of the world.

- ◆ Ask a learner:

    What's your name?
    Where are you from?
    Where were you born?

- ◆ Write the above information on a **Post-It™** note. Give the note to the learner and ask him or her to put the **Post-It™** note on his or her native country.
- ◆ Ask the group:

    What's his (or her) name?
    Where is he (she) from?
    Where was he (she) born?

- ◆ Have the first learner ask the same three questions of another learner while you continue to write the information on a **Post-It™** note.
- ◆ Continue until everyone in the class has a **Post-It™** note on the world map.

Handout 1-A is a spelling and clarification activity.
Extension Activity #1 is a discussion about the kinds of questions people ask when they are first introduced to each other.

- ◆ Divide learners into mixed ability groups.
- ◆ Have learners discuss and write a list of appropriate and inappropriate questions to ask when first introduced in their native countries.
- ◆ Debrief groups using **stand up and share** (see Glossary on page xx).

Handout 1-B is a categorizing activity. Learners work in pairs or small groups and decide together which questions are polite to ask in U.S. society and which are impolite.

IN YOUR COMMUNITY

Before learners complete this section of the worktext, play **Story Clip #1**.

STORY CLIP #1
TIME CODE: 2:05–2:35   **COUNTER TIMES:**
SCENE: Mr. Brashov's chef quits on opening day.
FIRST LINE: MR. BRASHOV: Did you forget to cook this? It tastes like it's raw.
LAST LINE: MR. BRASHOV: Go on, go on—you come back in one month. We will see who is right.

The chef doesn't think the café will last one month. Mr. Brashov tells him to come back. Ask learners to **predict** what the chef will find if he comes back in a month.

ASK AND ANSWER

HANDOUT 1-A

Practice spelling your classmates' names and the names of their native countries. Ask the questions below. Write the answers on the lines.

QUESTIONS TO ASK: *"What is your name?"*   *"How do you spell it?"*
                   "Where are you from?"   *"How do you spell it?"*

EXAMPLE: A: *What is your name?*   B: *My name is Jamal.*
                A: *How do you spell it?*   B: *J-A-M-A-L*
                A: *Could you repeat that?*   B: *Sure. J-A-M-A-L*

	NAME	NATIVE COUNTRY
1.		
2.		
3.		
4.		
5.		
6.		
7.		
8.		
9.		
10.		
11.		
12.		
13.		
14.		
15.		

The Crossroads Café Partner's Guide

The *Partner's Guide* is a small book that a formal tutor, a relative, a friend, a coworker, or a neighbor can use to help a learner improve his or her English. This little guide explains, in simple, direct language, what the "helper" can do to make learning with each episode of *Crossroads Café* even better for the learner. The guide provides one page of special instructions for each episode, as well as some general suggestions for a predictable yet lively approach to working with the learner. People who have never taught and seasoned tutors will find a wealth of hints in the *Partner's Guide* for helping learners succeed with their English.

The Crossroads Café Reproducible Master Packet

For the tutor who is working with more than one learner of *Crossroads Café,* the same 104 reproducible masters that are part of the *Teacher's Resource Books* are available separately. The masters can also be used by tutors who want to maximize a single learner's opportunities for interaction by working through the communicative activities in a learning-partner role with the student.

Index